AF530922

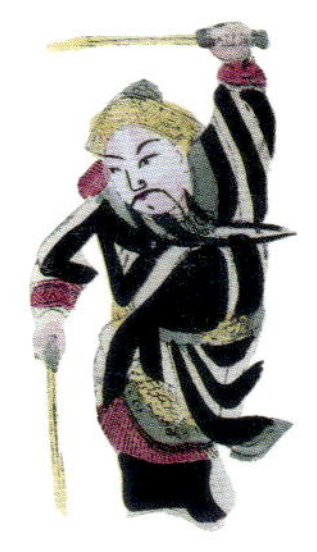

Chinese Festivals

New Year Paintings and Holiday Celebrations

Lusheng Pan & Jialu Tang

LONG RIVER PRESS
San Francisco

Editorial Committee
Art Adviser: Yang Xin, Wang Qingzheng & Zhang Daoyi
Chief Editor: Wu Shiyu
Deputy Chief Editor: Ma Ronghua & Dai Dingjiu
Editorial Committee Members: Qian Gonglin, Lin Lanying, Zhang Debao & Wu Shaohua

Author: Pan Lusheng & Tang Jialu
Executive Editor: Dai Dingjiu
Designer: Lu Quangen
Introduction: Zheng Tuyou
Translator: Ding Shaohong & Li Shanshan
English Editor: Luo Dayou
Series Editor: Chris Robyn

First edition 2004

ISBN 1-59265-016-3

Library of Congress Cataloging-in-Publication Data

Pan, Lusheng.
[Nian hua. English]
Chinese festivals : New Year paintings and holiday celebrations / Pan Lu sheng, Tang Jia lu.— 1st ed.
p. cm.
ISBN 1-59265-016-3 (hardcover)
1. Color prints, Chinese—Themes, motives. 2. New Year decorations, etc.—China. 3. Folk art—China. I. Tang, Jialu. II. Title.
NE1300.8.C6P365 2004
760'.04493942614'0951—dc22

2004007396

Published in the United States of America by
Long River Press
3450 3rd St., #4B, San Francisco, CA 94124
www.longriverpress.com
in association with Shanghai People's Fine Arts Publishing House

Printed in China

10 9 8 7 6 5 4 3 2 1

Table of Contents

Introduction

Festivals are a major part of understanding Chinese history, culture, and folk art. Festivals originated as an ancient form of divination, ancestor, or nature worship, and today they have developed into customs, gatherings, and activities which resonate throughout society—in China as well as in Chinese communities abroad.

This book deals primarily with Chinese New Year Paintings as an illustrative art. New Year Paintings, which are prevalent throughout China, share a rich history and a distinctive cultural style, utilizing the techniques of woodblock printing.

1. History and Development

*I*n Chinese folklore, the "Kitchen God," or "Door God" are the originators of New Year festival pictures. The origin of these pictures can be traced back to the mastery of the use of fire and the origins of the kitchen. Similarly, while the kitchen represented the life force of the people, the door was a portal to the outside, or the unknown. The door could help the people to repel evil, avert calamity, and aid in the protection of their families.

An ancient record in *The Funeral Costumes in the Records of Rites* recounts worshipping of the Door God, stating simply: "You offer the dishes to show respect to the Door God." Although there was no concrete image for the Door God in pre-dynastic China, during the Han Dynasty, portraits of Shen Tu, Yu Lei, and Cheng Qing appeared to exorcise evil, welcome auspiciousness, pray for blessings, and shun calamity. The origins of these figures can be traced to the following citation from the famous historical work, *The Book of Mountains and Seas*: "There is a huge mountain in the middle of the sea. On the top of the mountain grows a tremendous peach tree, which extends for a thousand miles. Among the branches from the east to the west is a Ghost Door. Thousands of ghosts go in and out of this door. There are two immortals in the heaven, whose names are Shen Tu and Yu Lei. Together they are responsible for the management of these ghosts. If any ghost committed any evil, it would be tied by weed rope and be thrown to feed the tiger. When the Yellow Emperor ascended the throne, he taught people how to exorcize the evil ghosts by drawing Shen Tu, Yu Lei, and a Tiger on the door. If any evil ghost invaded, it would be caught and be fed to the tiger."

By the end of Han Dynasty (206 B.C.-A.D. 220), there were numerous historical citations about the stories of Shen Tu and Yu Lei. Moreover, in *The Biography of the Thirteenth King of Jin in the History of Han*, it is also recorded that "Yue, King of Hui of Guangchuan, posted a picture of Cheng Qing in the image of a warrior with a sword in hand on the door of his palace. Historian Yan Shigu had a note saying that Cheng Qing was an ancient warrior. Warrior images appeared in the later Door-God paintings. The Door God and Door-God paintings are direct predecessors of New Year paintings.

In the Wei, Jin, and Southern and Northern Dynasties periods (220-589), the rooster picture on the door became a new style of door painting. In the *Record of the State of Chu* by Zong Lin, it is stated: "On the first day of the first lunar month, people post rooster pictures on the door, hung weed ropes above the picture, and placed a peach wood charm beside it, to scare away ghosts." There were also records about posting rooster pictures on the door in well known literature such as Yang Jia's *Records of Omissions*, which appeared during the Jin Dynasty (265-420).

Buddhism flourished during the Tang Dynasty (618-907) when temples and grottoes could be found everywhere in villages, towns, forests, and mountains. Door paintings were even found on the doors of kitchens, storerooms, and sitting rooms in various temples throughout the countryside. It was described in later records by Feng Yingjing: "The themes of recent door pictures include generals, courtiers, ancient wine cups, deer, bats, spiders, supernatural horses, bottles, and saddles. All of them carried names with auspicious meaning."

At the same time, the Chung K'uei Paintings became one of the themes for New Year Paintings for exorcising evil and shunning calamity. Shen Kuo of the Song Dynasty (960-1279) had detailed records on Chung K'uei Paintings in his work, *Replenishment.* In the fifth year of the reign of the Song Emperor Xining (1072), painters were ordered to copy and engrave printing plates with posters of Chung K'uei. On the eve of the New Year, the emperor ordered official painter Liang Kai to present the portraits of Chung K'uei. Such is the earliest record concerning wood-block painting of Chung K'uei in Chinese history.

Wood-block printing was an important condition for the widespread emergence of New Year paintings. The impression of Buddhist figures made during the period of Emperors Kaiyuan and Tianbao (713-755) in the Tang Dynasty were found in the famous Mogao Grottos of Dunhuang, and showed that the technique of wood-block printing had developed to a certain high level at that time. However, it was not until the Song Dynasty when wood-block techniques were used to print New Year paintings. The Northern Song Dynasty (960-1127) experienced an ascending economy, so the material and spiritual livelihood of the citizens inspired the form and development of wood-block New Year paintings. Thus, the overall level of art in terms of aesthetics and quality had been, as whole, enhanced considerably.

Song Emperor Hui Zong (r. 1110-1125) loved painting and he founded an imperial art academy to promote the development of painting as a discipline. At the same time, the painting of art had gradually found approval among the common people. Certain imperial artists, such as Su Hanchen and Li Song, also produced a great number of paintings about folk customs, such as *Baby Playing, Street Vendor, Auspicious, Five Kinds of Auspiciousness, Acrobatics Entertaining Children, Pilgrimage*, etc. There also appeared a group of famous folk painters, such as Liu Zongdao from the imperial capital of Kaifeng, Yang Wei from Jiangzhou of Shanxi, and Chen Tan from Jinyang. Zhao Loutai excelled at drawing towers, and Du Hai'er specialized in drawing children. Once these artists completed a painting, hundreds of copies would be printed for sale to the general public. This method was continued to be used until the early 20th century.

The form and development of New Year paintings also shared a close relationship with scholarly paintings of the Song Dynasty. At that time, there were no distinctive gaps between palace artists and folk painters. Paintings by famous artists were also displayed in public places such as teahouses, restaurants, medicinal and apothecary shops, and food markets to attract customers. Even the Imperial Art Academy bought paintings by folk painters depicting children and country life for ceremonial use within the imperial palace.

In terms of thematic imagery, imperial artists were particularly skilled at depicting flowers, birds, animals, or landscapes, while folk painters practiced mainly Taoist and Buddhist figures, houses, water scenes, buildings, and scenes and characters from popular folk stories.

In the Song Dynasty, there were both hand-drawn New Year paintings and wood-block prints, but the superiority of wood block techniques was clearly superior, as more than one thousand copies could be done from one run. Wood-block printing was actually de-

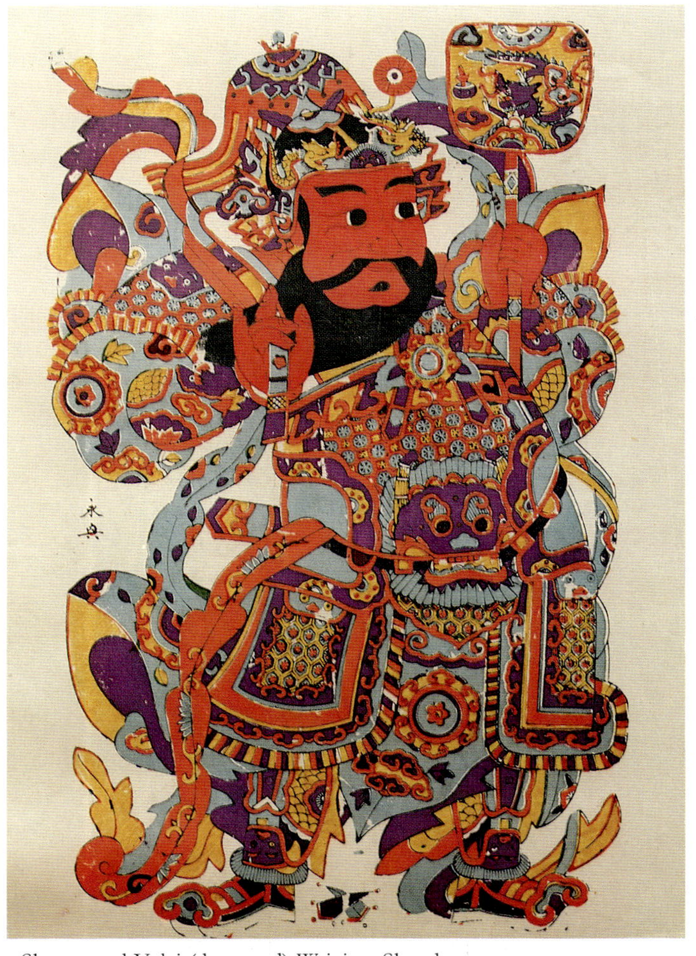

Shentu and Yulei (door-god) Weixian, Shandong

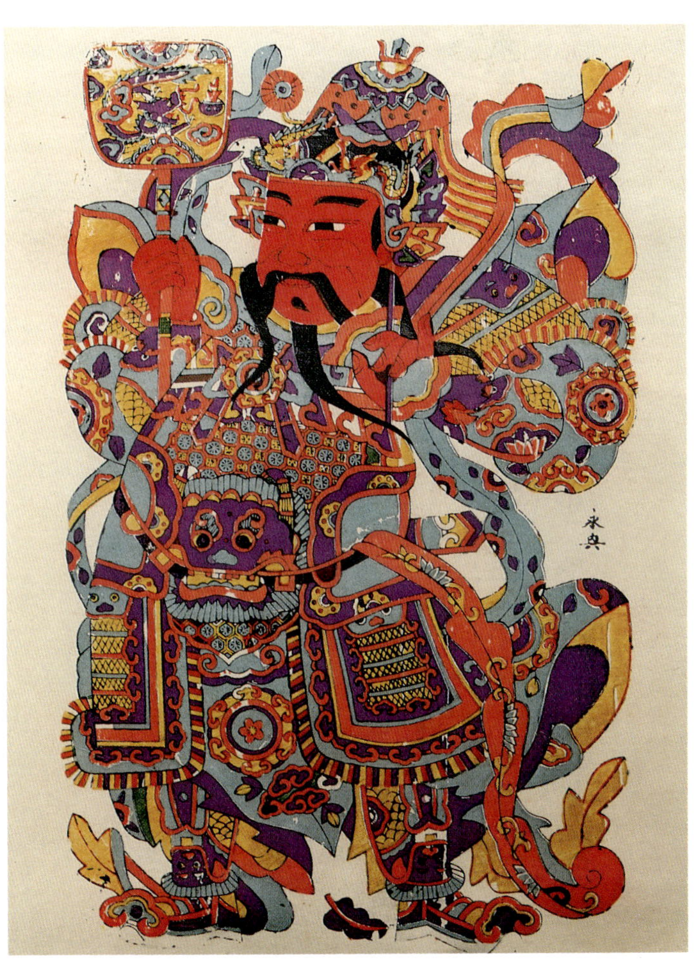

Shentu and Yulei (door-god), Weixian, Shandong

veloped from the form of "Paper Horse" (or "Holly Horse") printing. The Paper Horse technique was known as a form of engraving and printing of Buddhist images and sutras during the Tang Dynasty. By the Song Dynasty, Paper Horse prints were no longer only printed and given out by temples with the donations from Buddhist believers. They were also printed and sold to the general populace. Those shops which specialized in Paper Horse also printed and sold prints of Buddhist images. In anticipation of the New Year, they also produced copies of Chung K'uei, Fortune Horse, Looking-back Horse, Peachwood Charm, Tiger Head, and Door-God pictures. The scenes of the buying and selling of New Year paintings in the Song capital were

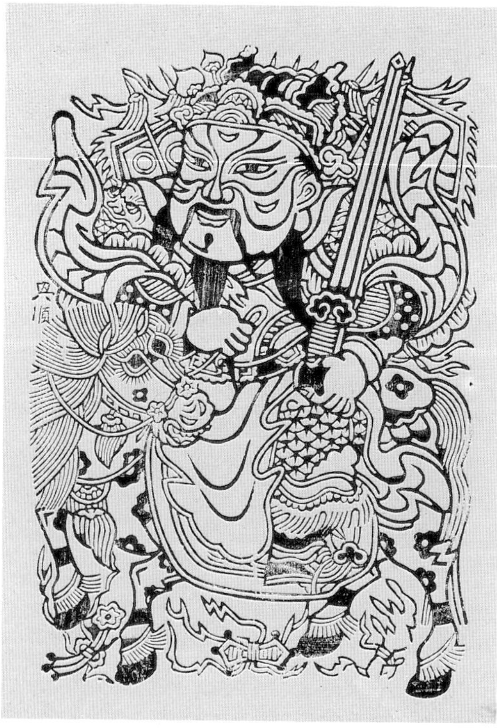

Riding Horse with Whip (warrior door-god), Zhuxian Town, Kaifeng, Henan

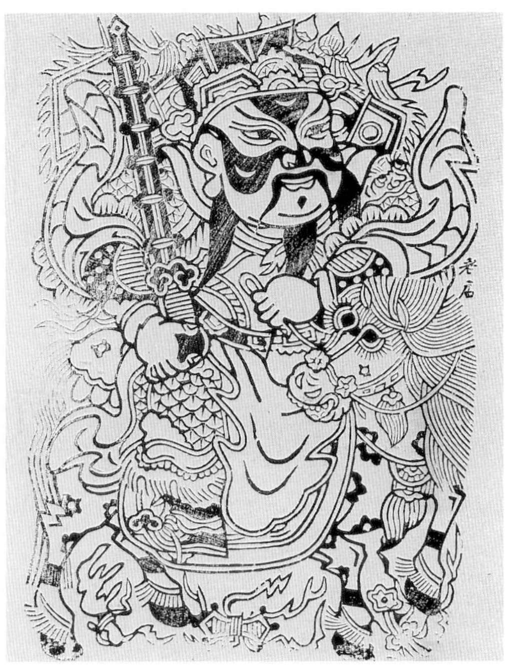

Riding Horse with Whip (warrior door-god), Zhuxian Town, Kaifeng, Henan

described in many books, such as *Records of Dreams* by Wu Zimu, *Prosperity in the Capital* by Meng Yuanlao, and *Old Stories of Wulin* by Zhou Mi. The themes of the New Year paintings were not limited only to images of Door Gods Shen Tu and Yu Lei, or roosters, tigers, or peach-wood charms, but had been extended to include Chung K'uei, Fortune Horse, Looking-back Horse and many images. The hanging of New Year Paintings had become a custom among the common folk, reaching the height of their popularity during the Song Dynasty.

When Song Emperor Gao Zong moved the capital to the south and established the Southern Song Dynasty (1127-1279), some painters in the capital Bianliang moved south to Lin'an (today 's Hangzhou in Zhejiang Province), while others moved to Pingyang (today 's Linfen in Shanxi Province). Still others went to Zhuxian Town in Henan.

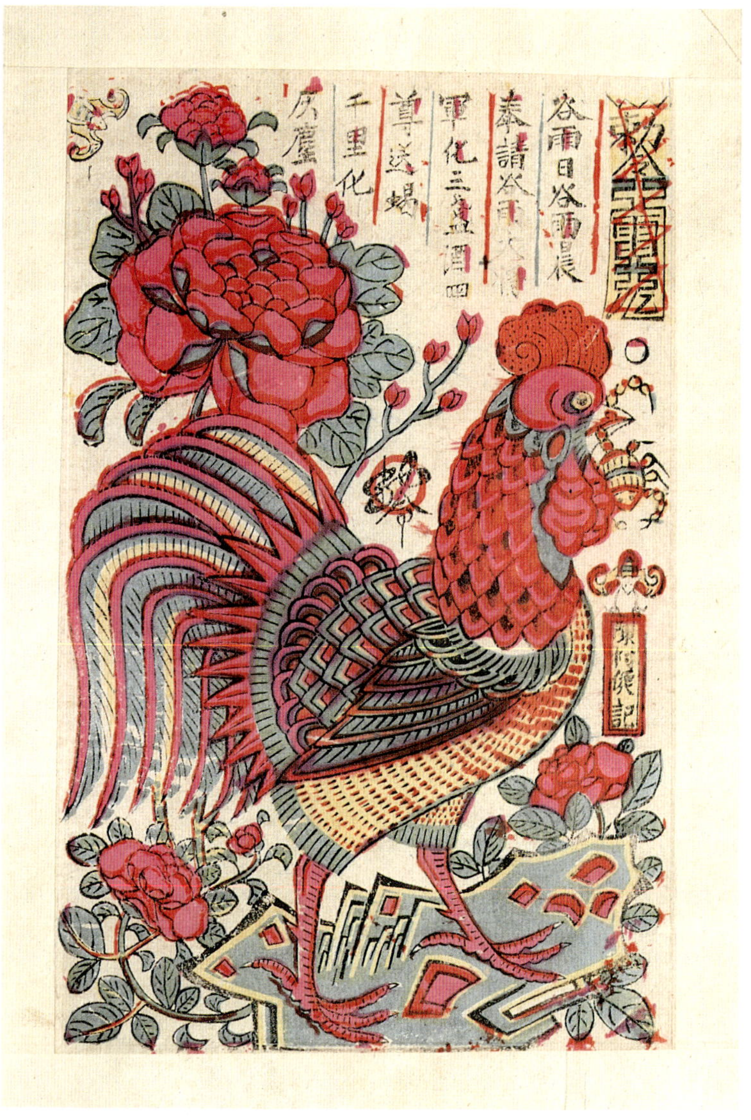

Rooster (wood engraving), Fengxiang, Shaanxi

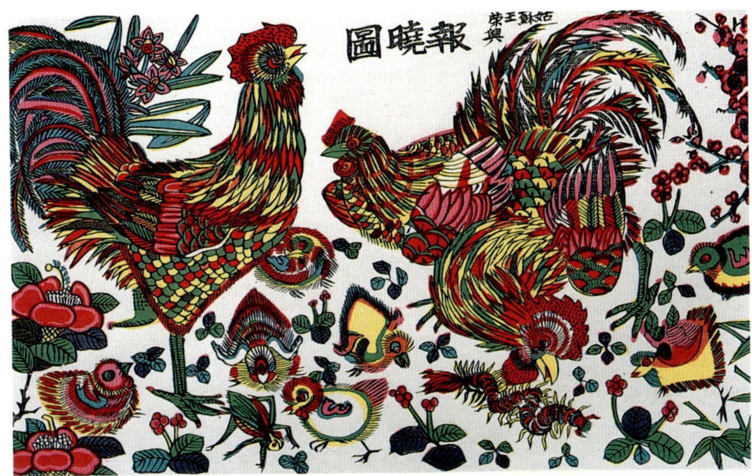

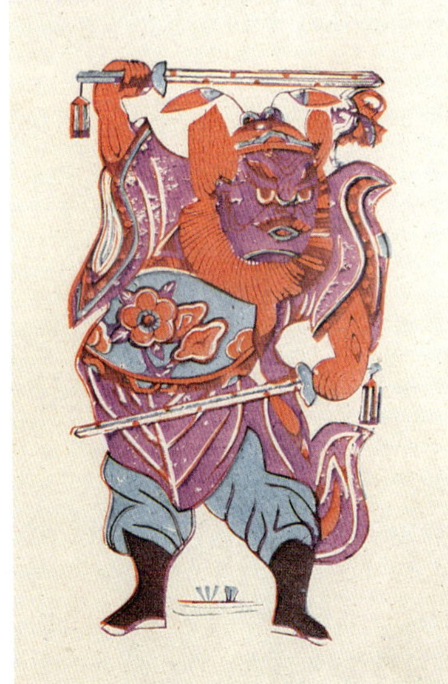

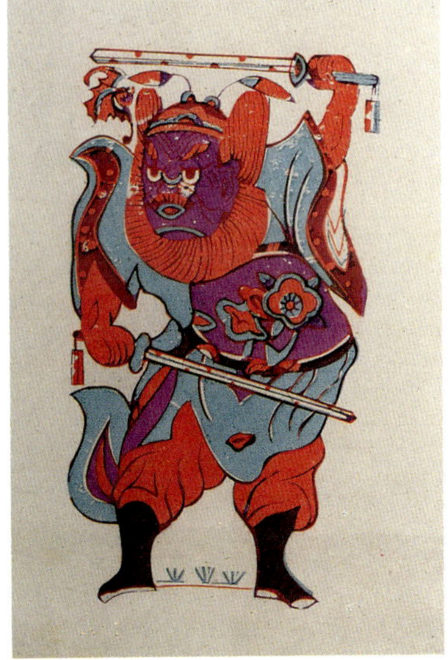

Top: Heralding Daybreak, Taohuawu, Suzhou
Bottom right: Beating Pig Ghost (door-god), Weixian, Shandong
Bottom left: Beating Pig Ghost (door-god), Weixian, Shandong

Together, these painters helped to establish several major production bases of New Year paintings, many of which are still well known and prosperous printing regions even today. In the Southern Song Dynasty, wood-block printing reached a further development, with many more varieties available. Door-God pictures, for example, were now produced in more sizes and more styles than ever before. The largest one could be life size, as tall as a person. Yuan Jiong described the New Year painting styles of Northern Song in his *Reading by the Window*: "In Bianliang, the Door-God had many styles with Tiger-head helmet, while the gates of noble families were all decorated in gold." Similar descriptions could also be found in Li Song's *Year's Paintings*. On the front gate of houses of noble families was a military Door-God picture and on the gate of their inner central hall was posted a Door-God in the image of a civil official in court dress.

Nowadays it is very hard to find even a piece of these types of New Year paintings of the Southern Song Dynasty, but their styles could be seen in those of later years during the Liao and Kin period (916-1234).

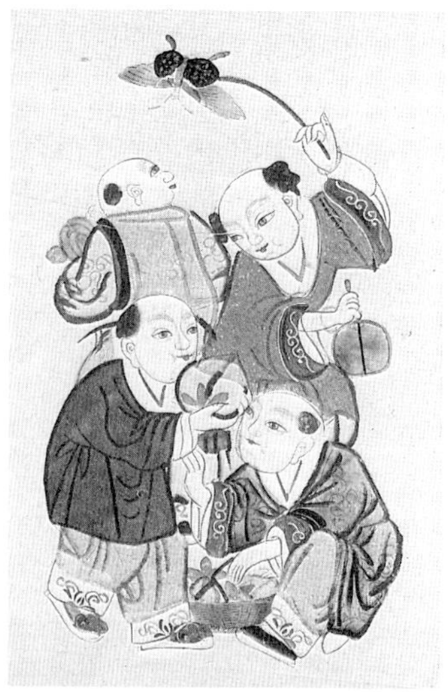

Four Happiness (door-picture), Mianzhu, Sichuan

Four Happiness (door-picture), Mianzhu, Sichuan

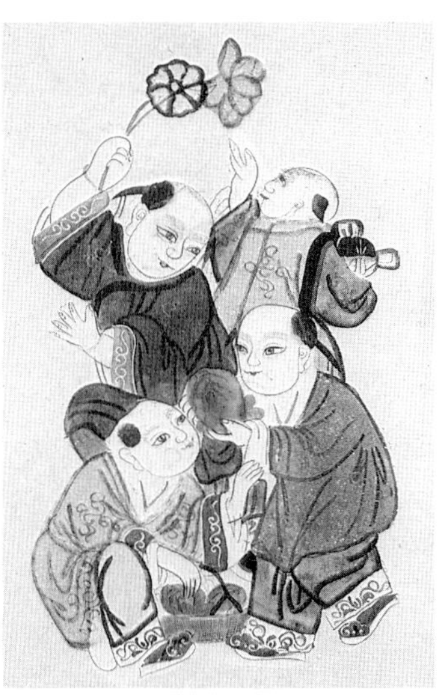

During the Liao and Kin period (916-1234), the production sites of wood-block printing in northern China were Pingyang, Yingxian and Datong, located in Shanxi Province; and Beijing. From the wood-block print *Four Beauties* and Paper Horse picture *Brave King of Wu'an* produced in Pingyang, the high quality of wood-block printing in Southern Song Dynasty can be easily seen. The work *Four Beauties* was comprised of the portraits of Wang Zhaojun, Zhao Feiyan, Ban Ji, and Lu Zhu. The Chinese characters for "unmatched beauties" were printed on the painting, and below that was another line: "engraved and printed by the Ji Family of Pingyang." The work entitled *Brave King of Wu'an* features a portrait of Lord Guan, with a line reading: "Throne of Lord Wu'an" and another line: "Printed by the Xu Family of Pingyang." Both of these works are some of the best examples of wood-block due to their superb engraving skills, vivid images, and attention to detail.

The multiple wood-block color print *Stealing Peaches* found in the Forest of Steles in Xi'an was another fine representative work, this time with a birthday celebration as its central theme. It shows that

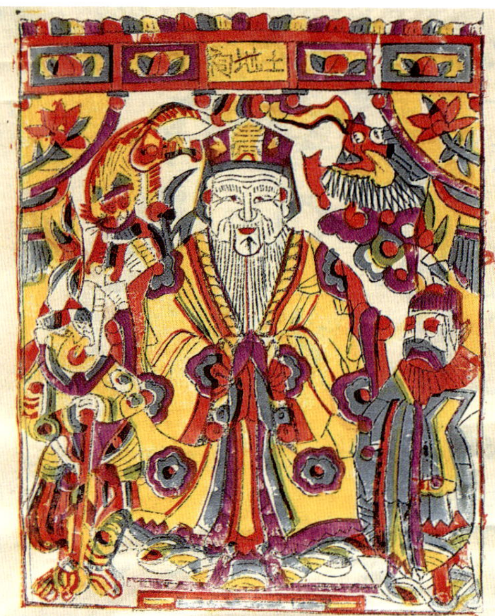

Land God, Fengxiang, Shaanxi

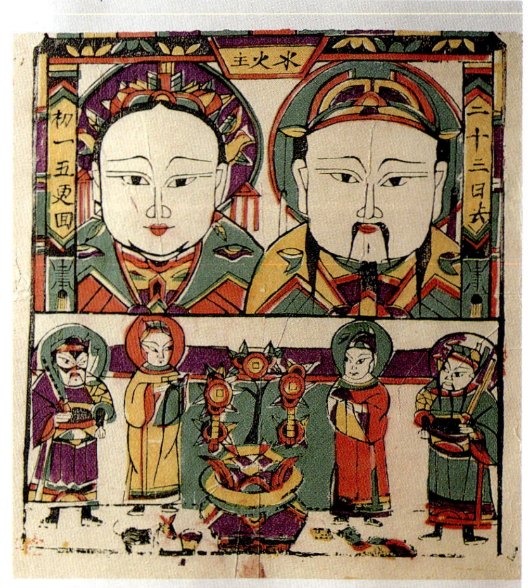

Kitchen God and River God, Zhuxian Town, Kaifeng, Henan

Kitchen God,
Linfen, Shanxi

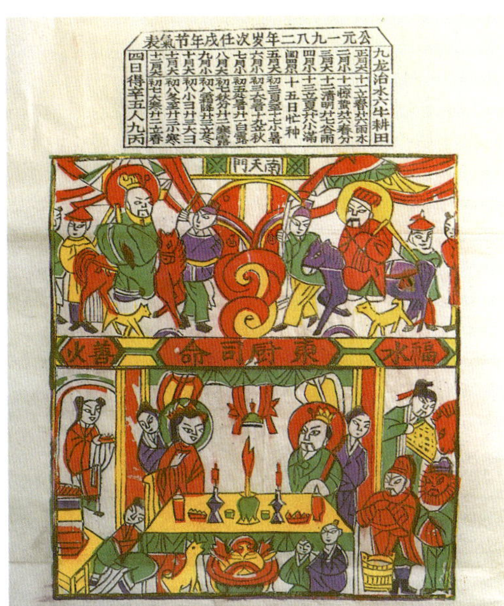

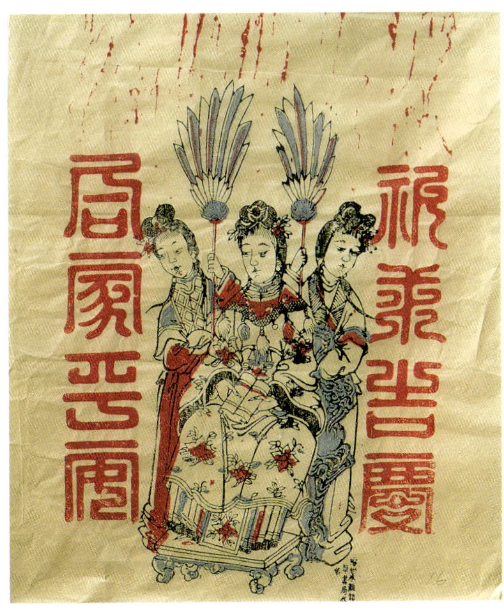

Wishing Auspiciousness
and Peace, Sichuan

wood -block color printing had matured by the 12th and 13th centuries and was already popular among the people with a wide variety of themes and styles.

New Year wood-block printing, which originated in central China, had spread to southern Chinese provinces such as Jiangsu and Fujian, with Hangzhou in Zhejiang Province serving as the center of production in the Southern Song Dynasty. In northern China, wood-block printing encompassed Pingyang in Shanxi and spread north to Beijing, as well as to Shaanxi, Hebei, and Shandong provinces. In Sichuan Province in southwestern China, wood-block printing formed since the Tang Dynasty had not been influenced by styles from other parts of the country, where it retained its unique style known as Mianzhu, with images of the Door-God as its central theme.

The Song Dynasty was a period that had not only laid a foundation for the development of New Year paintings but also was a thriving period in the history of Chinese New Year paintings.

The Mongol, or Yuan Dynasty, had a short life of less than a hundred years, and during this period the "Gongbi" style (the style of painting which emphasized realism) began to decline. Thusly, New Year paintings were also by this time on the wane.

During the Yuan Dynasty, paintings depicting daily life were fewer in number and were seldom mentioned in official records. For the most part, New Year paintings simply followed the existing styles of the Song, such as the work *Street Vendor* by Wang Zhenpeng, and *Playing with Children in Spring* and *Good News* by an anonymous artist. There were also new styles of paintings created and used by later generations of artists, such as the calendar painting *Winter Season*, whose style is imitated even today. *Farming and Weaving* is representative of another popular theme in Yuan Dynasty folk art, as described in poems and inscriptions of that time. *Ten Busy Things of Men, Ten Busy Things of Women*, and *Happy Family Reunion at New Year Festival* were all representative paintings of the theme. In Beijing, workshops that produced and sold Paper Horse suddenly appeared. Printing using the Paper Horse technique was carried on until the end of the Qing Dynasty.

After the founding of the Ming Dynasty (1368-1644), commercial and handicraft industries experienced a new level of flourishing development, and the prosperity of the handicraft industry facilitated the renaissance of the art of New Year paintings in technique and material supply. The use of illustrations in novels and in opera scripts also promoted the development of wood-block painting, and especially the improvement of engraving techniques. From the examples collected from this period, the themes, engraving skills, and artistic styles of New Year paintings of Ming Dynasty had become very diversified. Though diverse, the styles and forms tended to become set, and the themes experienced relatively continuous evolution during the Ming Dynasty. Examples of famous artwork includes *Winter Seasons, Harmonious Atmosphere, South Pole Stars, God of Longevity, Eight Immortals Celebrating Birthday, Portraits of Chung K'uei, Picture of Piety,* and Paper Horse work, *Ten Kings*. There were also some New Year paintings drawn on silk which were of excellent quality and which demonstrated truly superb workmanship. Examples of these include: *Door-Gods Qin Qiong and Wei Chigong*, as well as the famous works entitled *One Hundred Auspicious Things, Best Wishes for All Ages,* and *One Hundred Deer Bring Longevity*. In the Ming Dynasty, there was now less emphasis placed on the traditional themes of stories about Daoist and Buddhist monks. Rather, artists turned to painting about folk customs and auspicious greetings due in large part by the patronage of the upper class. According to the records in *Hearings of the Classics* by Yu Jicheng, *Unofficial Accounts* by Zhu Yunming, and *Records of Consideration* by Liu Ruoyu, folk custom paintings, such as *Farming and Weaving, Beautiful Scenery in March*, and paintings describing the fighting career of Ming Emperor Tai Zu were displayed in the palace. These themes were very close to those depicted in regular New Year paintings, though the characters were often different. For example, the story about the rebellion lead by Tai Zu was also depicted in even present-day New Year paintings. During the Ming Dynasty there were more New Year paintings depicting celebrations and auspicious themes. This paralleled the increase in the celebration of birthdays, promotions, and anniversaries which became more prominent at this time in Chinese history, particularly among the gentry elite. By the end of the Ming, the technique of multiple wood-block use for color printing had matured, with the use of watermarking and embossed printing being applied to New Year Paintings. The workshops of Yangliuqing in Tianjin,

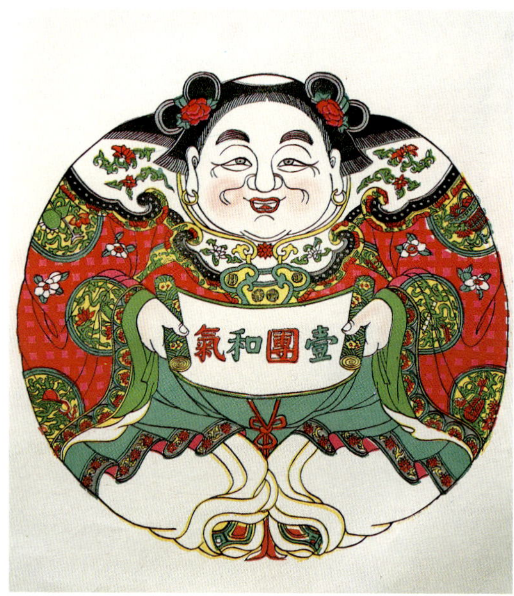

Harmonious Atmosphere, Taohuawu, Suzhou

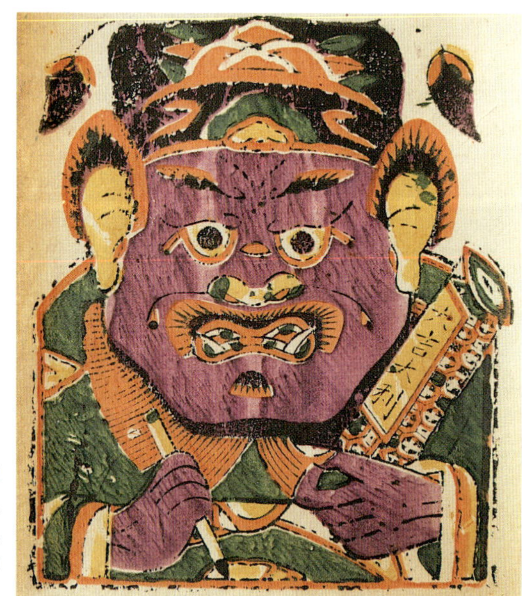

Chung K'uei' s Head Portrait (door-picture), Zhuxian Town, Kaifeng, Henan

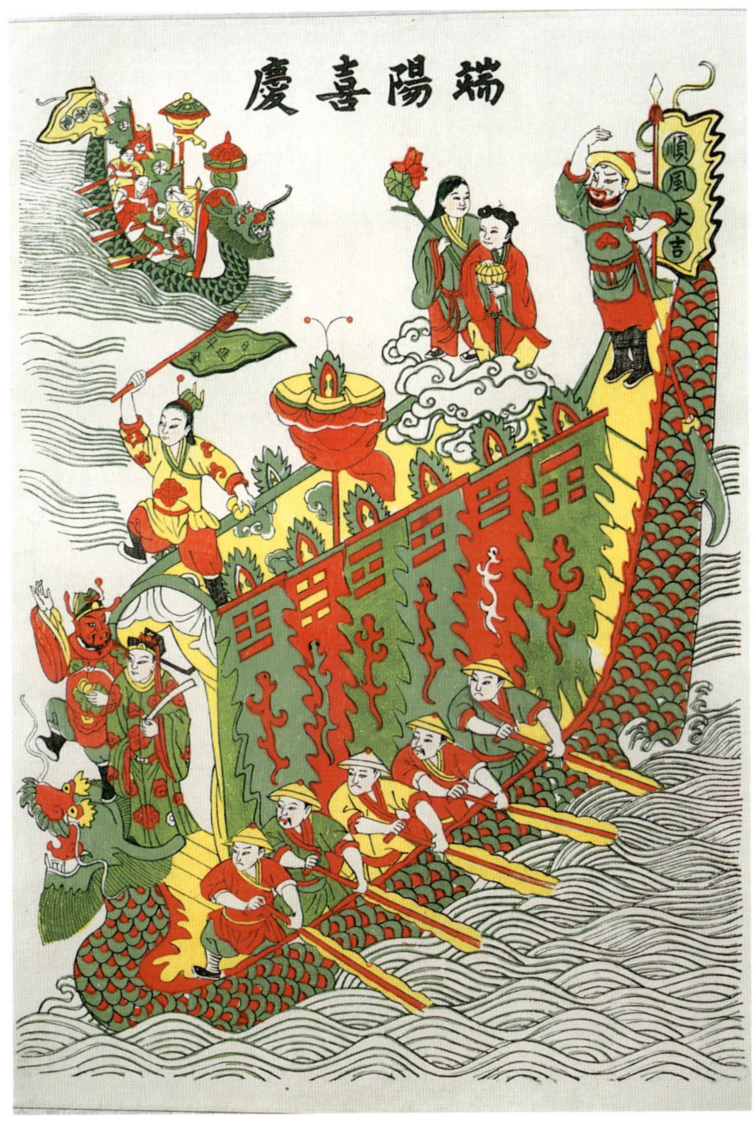

A happy Dragon Boat Festival, Suzhou

Yangjiabu in Weifang, Shandong, and Taohuawu, located in Suzhou, became especially well known for their New Year paintings during the Ming Dynasty.

Due to peasant uprisings and decades of war which characterized the end of the Ming Dynasty, however, many famous New Year painting workshops in Mianzhu, Chengdu, Suzhou, Nanjing, and Kaifeng, as well as many others, were destroyed and their wood-block plates and paintings burned. Most of the wood-block paintings existing in China today from this period are survivors from Suzhou, Beijing, Tianjin, and Shanxi.

In the Qing Dynasty (1644-1911), the printing of New Year paintings experienced further development and would enter a new era of prosperity after the downturn which marked the close of the Ming Dynasty. During the early Qing, the government adopted a series of new policies for social stability and economic development. During the reign of Emperor Kangxi (1662-1722) for instance, the state was prosperous and people lived in peace. New Year paintings at that time reflected this peaceful as well as the enhanced level of artistry which was subsequently displayed.

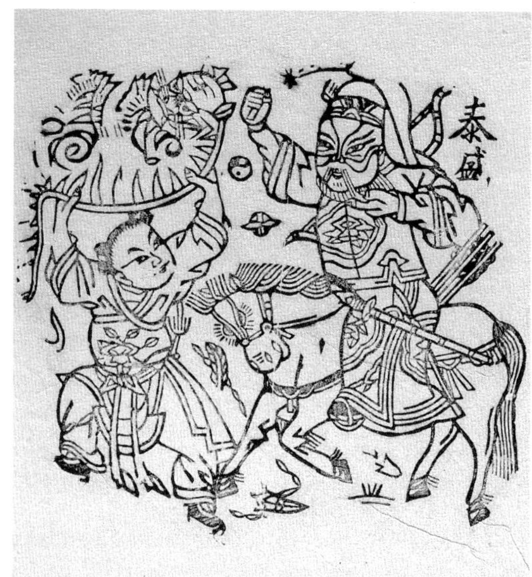

Flying Tiger Hill, Zhuxian Town, Kaifeng, Henan

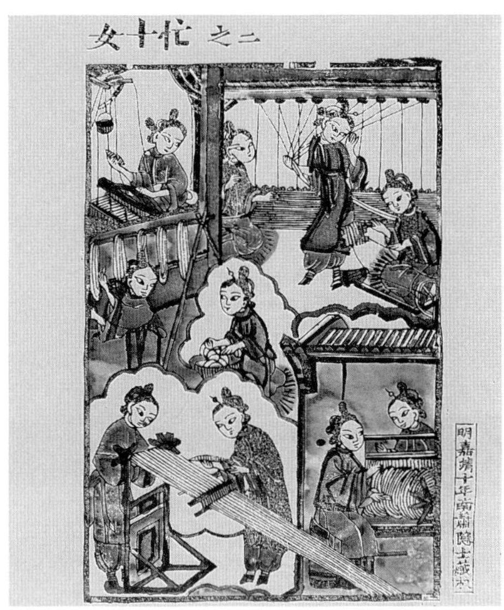

Ten Busy Things of Women, Fengxiang, Shaanxi

Themes became more diversified, including opera characters, characters from folk tales, birds, animals, and flowers, and, of course, landscapes. Artists found more forms and richer methods of expression, developing from the traditional strong-colored realistic painting techniques, to engraving, or joint printing and drawing. The images became more lively, and sometimes more decorative, romantic, fantastic, or imaginary. The carvings, some very delicate and some very bold, embodied different styles.

The painting store of Wangjunpu in Suzhou was opened during the late Ming/early Qing transition, and it only produced copies of works done in the old style. Later, as a result of social conditions during the early Qing, the shop began to display themes which explicitly encouraged the following of filial piety, having good neighborly relations, and a peaceful life with a prosperous business. Some of the best examples of this philosophy include the work, *Family Banner of Filial Piety,* and *Better Relations Between Friends and Relatives*. New themes were developed for opera stories and historical stories which were in

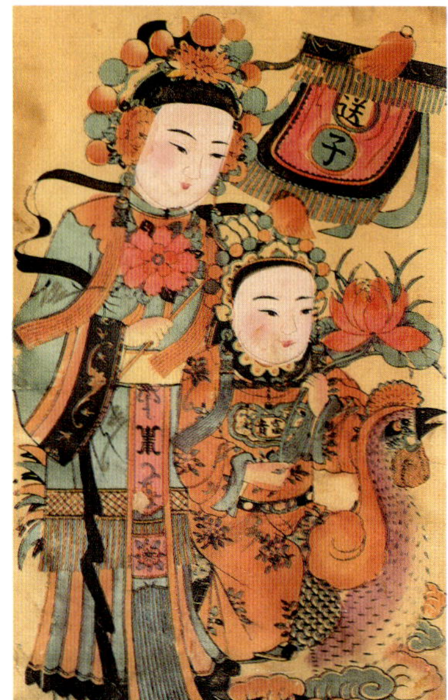

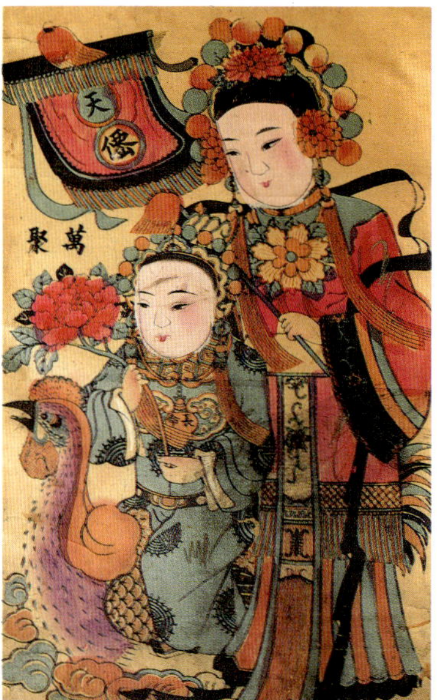

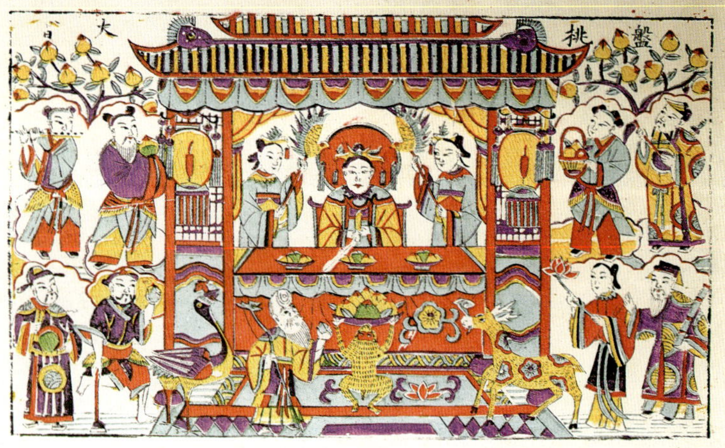

Top left: Qilin Delivering the Child, Gaomi, Shandon
Top right: Qilin Delivering the Child, Gaomi, Shandong
Bottom: A Banquet of Peach for Immortals, Weixian, Shandong

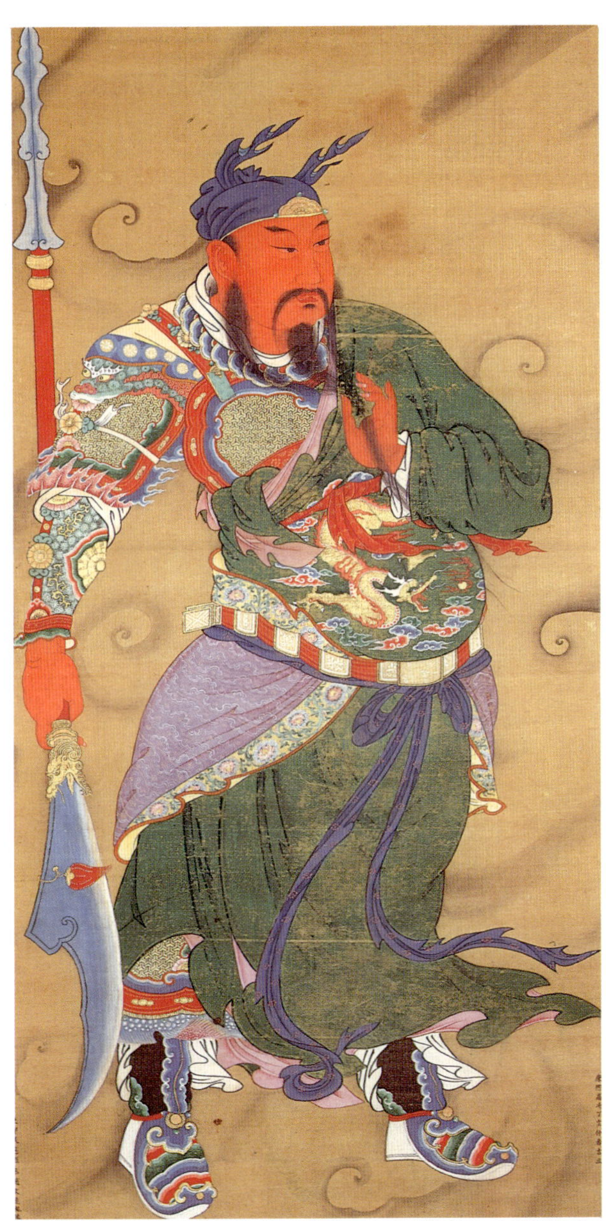

Lord Guan, a hero in the *Three Kingdoms,* worshiped in China.

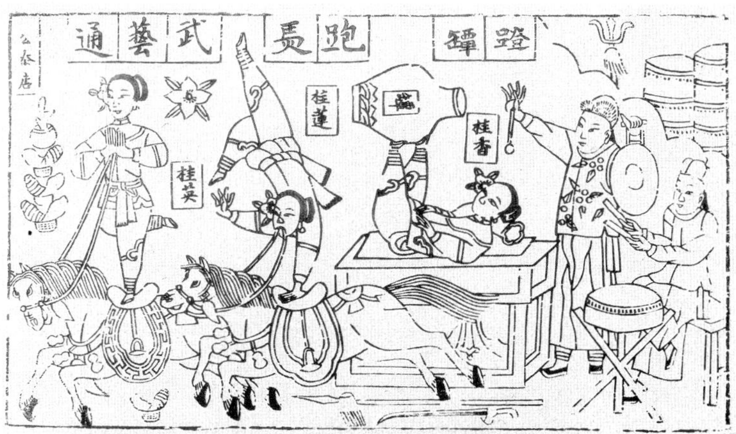

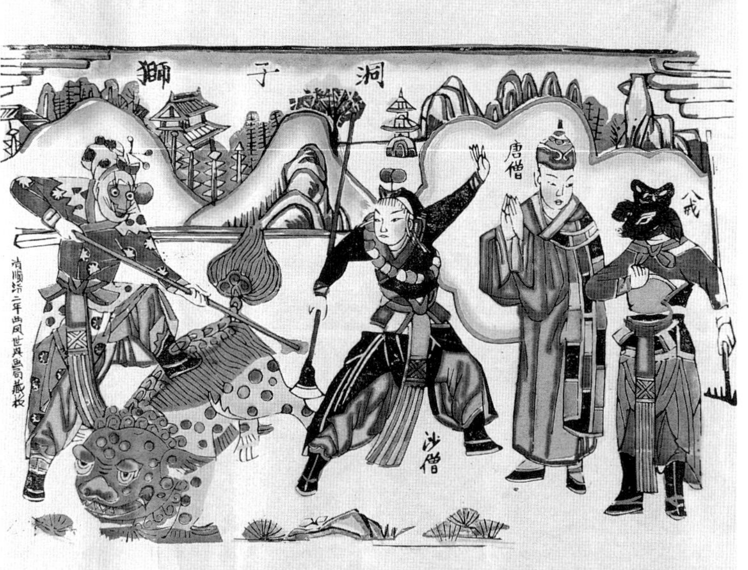

Top: Juggling the Jar with Feet and Riding a Horse, Weixian, Shandong
Bottom: Lion Cave, Fengxiang, Shaanxi

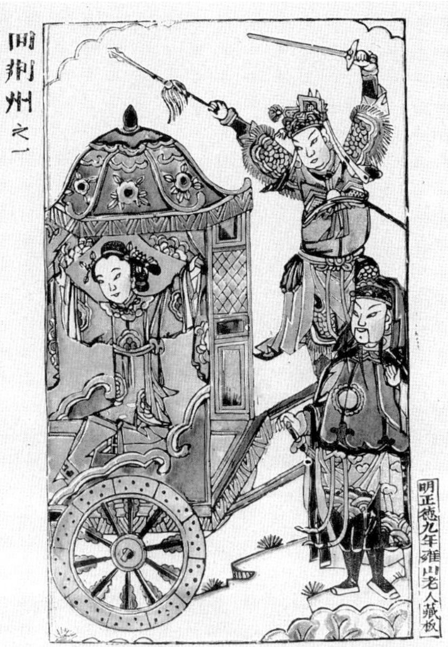

Back to Jingzhou, a scene from classical novel *Three Kingdoms*, Qishan, Shaanxi

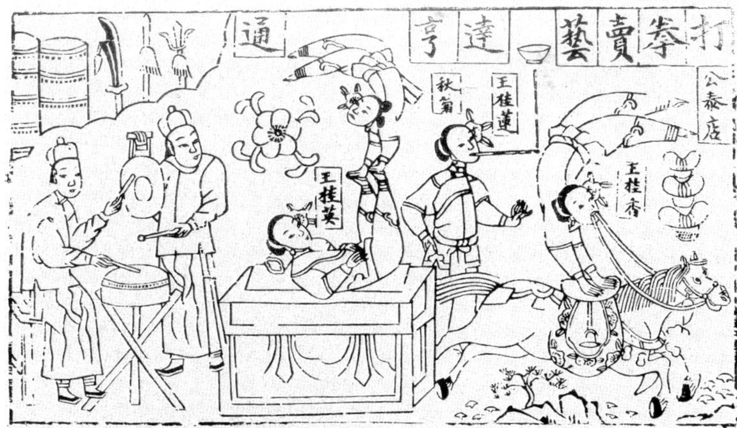

Acrobatic Performers, Weixian, Shandong

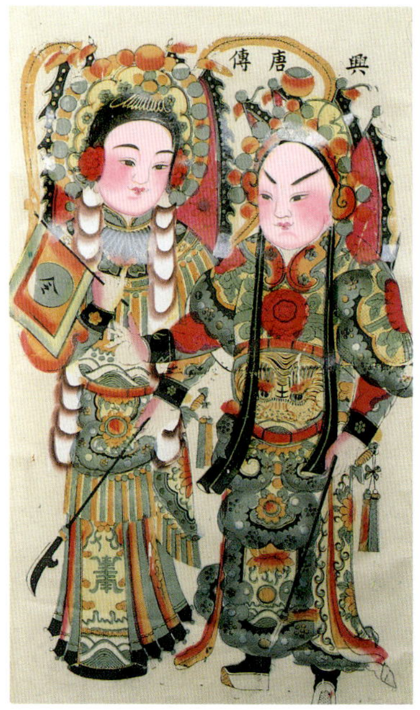

Combating Sanyin Battle Formation, Gaomi, Shandong

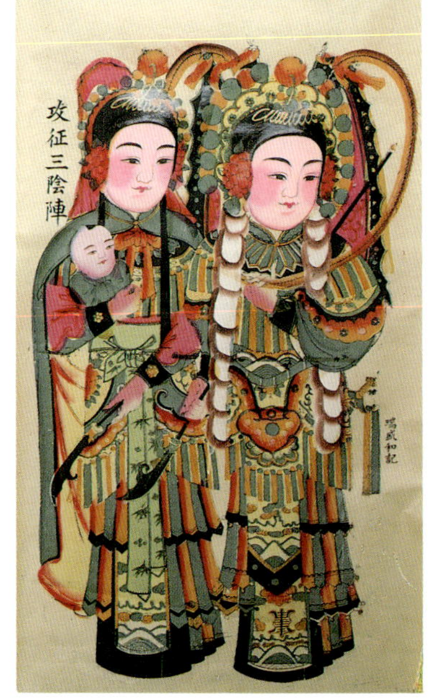

Combating Sanyin Battle Formation, Gaomi, Shandong

Door-God, Hekou, Yunnan

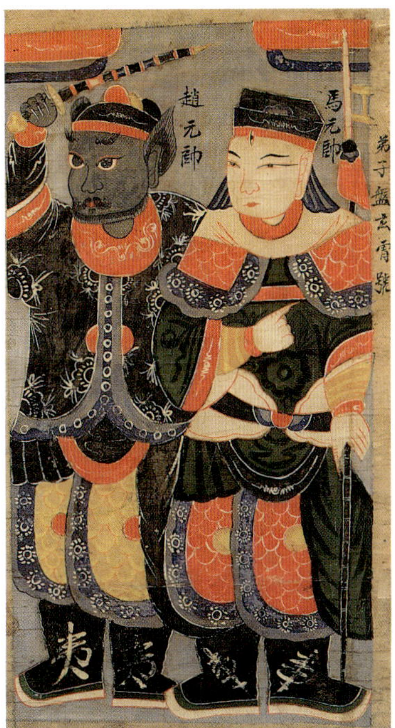

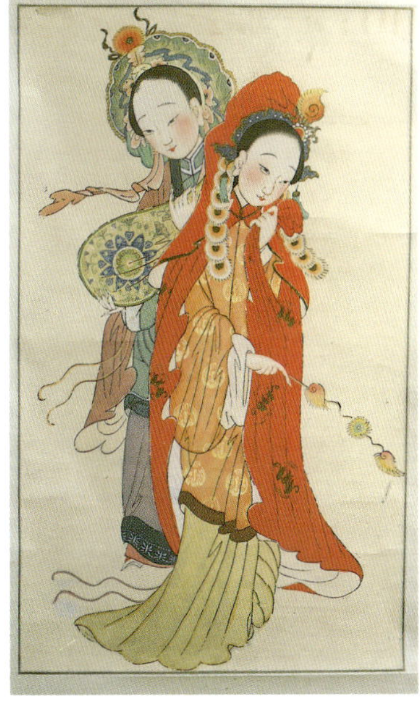

Wang Zhaojun Marries to the Western Region (Gongjian), Houma, Shanxi

turn well received by the people, such as *Twenty-eight Constellation Immortals Make Troubles in Kunyang.* The same themes could also be found in the New Year paintings produced by the Yangliuqing workshop. In addition, there also came new themes depicting peasant life, such as *Busy and Leisure*, and *Busy with Farming.* In the early Qing, old-style works depicting women with babies, children, Door-Gods, Chung K'uei, and pictures using Paper Horse techniques were kept in print by using existing old wood-block plates or by re-engraving certain other plates. New images of generals in Qing army uniforms began to appear in the New Year paintings produced by shops in Mianzhu, Sichuan, which were famous for their Door-God prints.

Popular novels rose to prominence in the early Qing even though they were banned by the government. However, the use and adaptation of fictional work provided an ideal source of inspiration for many New Year painting print shops. Many illustrators joined the rank of artists creating socially new and noteworthy paintings. Again, the New Year paintings had developed yet again in terms of theme or historical setting, whether depicting opera figures or characters in popular novels. Even the Yangliuqing, Suzhou, and Mianzhu workshops used large-size paper to print stories as a single image with a single, epic scene and dozens of figures depicted. Some paintings reflected the Ming loyalist movement and their revolt against the "foreign" Qing rulers.

New Year paintings enjoyed a great leap in terms of popularity during the reign of Qing Emperor Qianlong (1736-1795), considered one of the greatest of all Qing emperors. Many workshops now had newly engraved wood-block plates, and the prints made by Yangliuqing of Tianjin and Taohuawu of Suzhou were some of the most beautiful. Again, themes had been broadened, and existing styles further enriched. Western-style painting also flourished during this period, thus lending their influence to the creation of New Year paintings. In depicting cities and urban life, New Year paintings absorbed the techniques of three-dimensionality, perspective, and unique shading techniques used to similar effect in Western paintings of the period. This influence of Western painting was significant and can probably be traced to the Jesuit scholar Matteo Ricci who brought a consciousness of Western art to China in the late Ming; and by another

Jesuit artist, Giuseppe Castiglione, who served as a painter to the imperial court during the reign of Emperor Qianlong.

By the late Qing, however, the prosperity of the country was gone. As a result of war, peasant rebellion, and dynastic decline and corruption, the market for New Year paintings was steadily worsening. However, even in this period of dynastic decline, new titles and styles of New Year paintings were still emerging. In addition to traditional themes offered by historical stories, the publication of the classical novel *Hong Lou Meng*, more popularly known as *A Dream of Red Mansions*, once again offered a new and vibrant source for the creation of New Year paintings. Invasion by foreign armies during the 19th century also inspired patriotism among the people, and New Year paintings which depicted the struggle against imperialism also emerged, such as *Victory of the Sea War by Commander-in-chief Liu*; *Northern Expedition of Heavenly Kingdom Troops*; *Victory of Red River*; and *Burning the Seaside Building*.

Other paintings were a direct reflection of a newly-emerging modern China, works such as *Shanghai Railway Station*; *Abandon Opium*; *Marriage of Foreigners*; *Weaving and Spinning*; and *Girls' School.* Ever since the failed reform movement of 1898, many New Year paintings de-

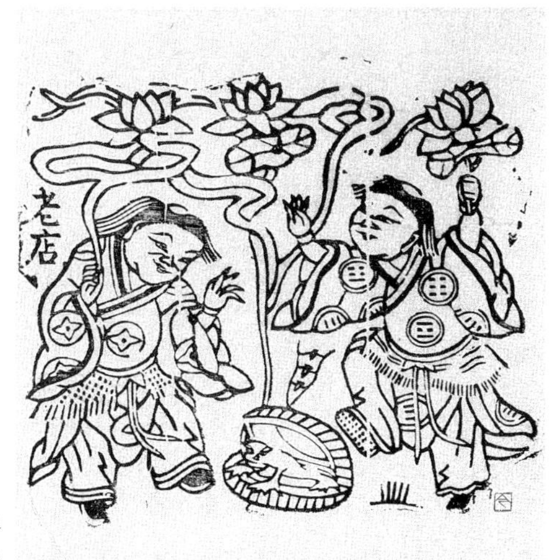

Two Immortals, Zhuxian Town, Kaifeng, Henan

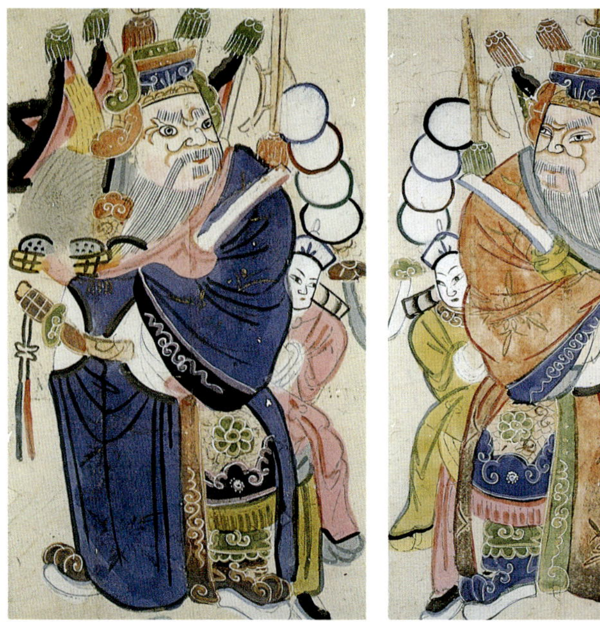

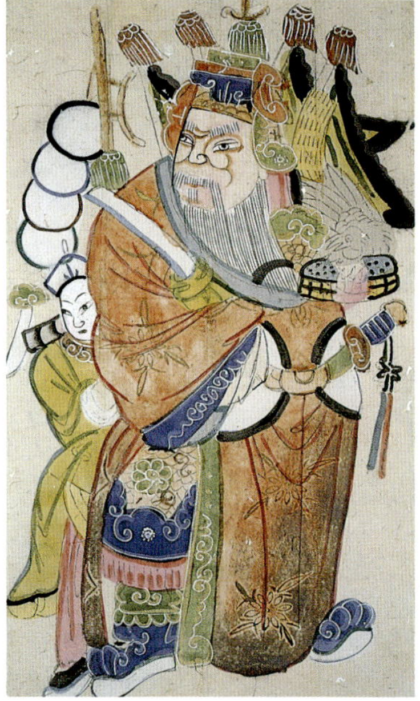

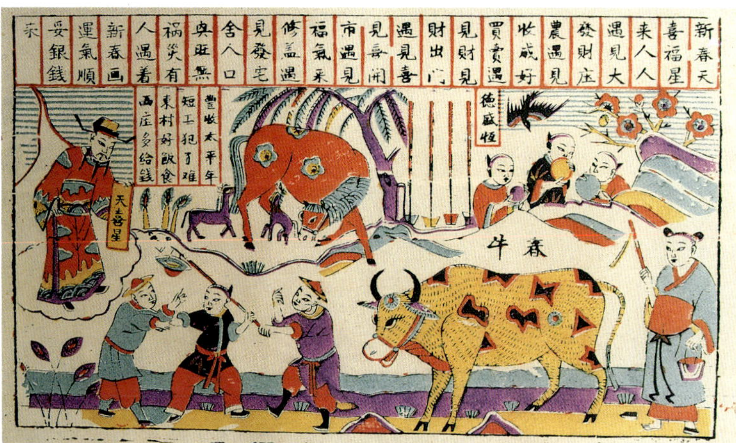

Top left: Door-picture, Mianzhu, Sichuan
Top right: Door-picture, Mianzhu, Sichuan
Bottom: Spring Cow, Henan

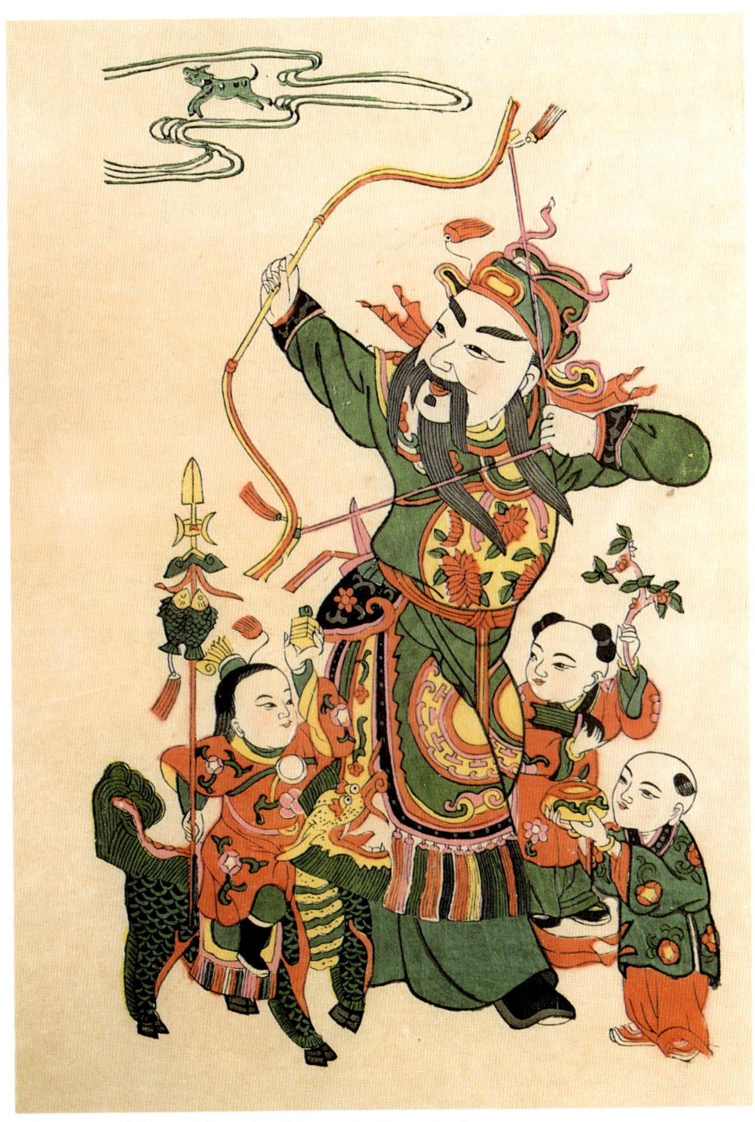

Immortal Zhang Shooting Heavenly Dog, Suzhou

picting themes of "reform" and an increased modern sensibility were produced. Often these took for their subject matter themes such as establishing new schools, raising women' s rights, studying new cultures, and advocating solidarity. Some well-known painters in Shanghai, Suzhou, Yangzhou, and Tianjin created many fine works with the themes of resisting foreign invasion while advocating patriotism. Among them were Qian Hui'an, Wu Youru, Tian Zilin, and Gao Tongxuan. Due to the use of modern printing technology and the introduction of Western aesthetics, New Year paintings began to be produced by modern lithographic printing rather than wood-block. Some works were printed with monthly calendars by combining realistic "Gongbi" techniques with charcoal and watercolor techniques commonly seen in Western art. These were mainly produced in Tianjin and Shanghai. Shanghai gradually became the main producer of New Year calendar paintings. These featured popular themes, such as opera stories, auspicious gatherings, as well as images of beautiful women. These calendar posters were the early form of popular culture posters commonly seen in urban China during the 1920s and 1930s.

2. Themes of New Year Paintings

New Year paintings have broad themes including all aspects of social life in China. They can be grouped into the following general categories:

Gods and immortals

Originally, the depiction of gods and immortals were the origins of New Year paintings, and had a dominant position within the marketplace since the inception of New Year paintings. The gods and immortals came from Buddhism, Daoism and Confucianism, as well as from folk stories and oral histories, including the *Three Heavenly Emperors, the Jade Emperor, Guanyin or Goddess of Mercy, the God of Land, the Kitchen God, Door God, God of Wealth, God of Fortune, God of Longevity, Chung K'uei, Dragon King, Lord Guan, the Eight Immortals, Goddess of the Sea (Mazu), God of the Road, God of the Bridge, Lord of Carpentry, Lu Ban, God of Medicine, Weaver Huang*, etc.

Gods and immortals worshipped by the people accounted for more than 300 figures, and those which commonly appeared in New Year paintings numbered over one hundred. New Year paintings depicting gods and immortals were posted on gates and doors, but most were enshrined indoors with fixed frames or niches. Paper Horse paintings were not posted, but only used for burning during ceremonial occasions. Paper Horse paintings often feature many more images of gods and immortals, and display genuine value as distinctive pieces of art.

The paintings also used magic symbols in such works as *Gods in Heaven and on Earth*; *Kitchen God; Chung K'uei Protects the House*; *God of Fire*, etc. Some magic symbols with characters and patterns were believed to have the function of repelling evil, such as the posters of *Eight Diagrams of Tai Ji, Precious Symbols for Safety, the Urgent Order*, etc.

Most New Year paintings which feature gods and immortals also contained religious or supernatural connotations, and for a very

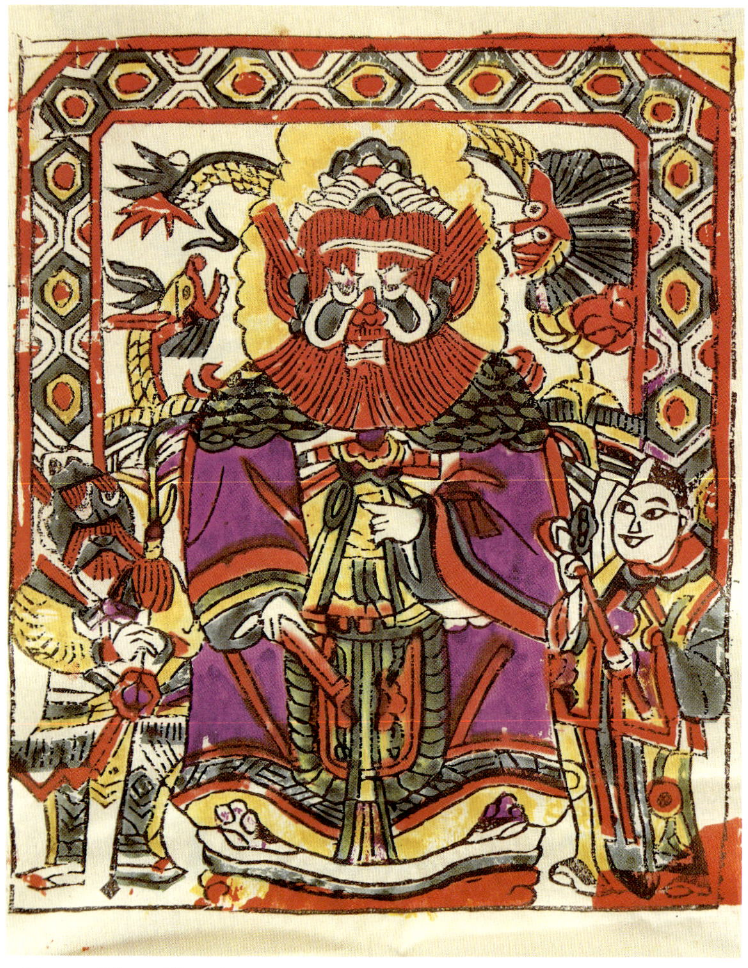

Dragon King, Shanxi

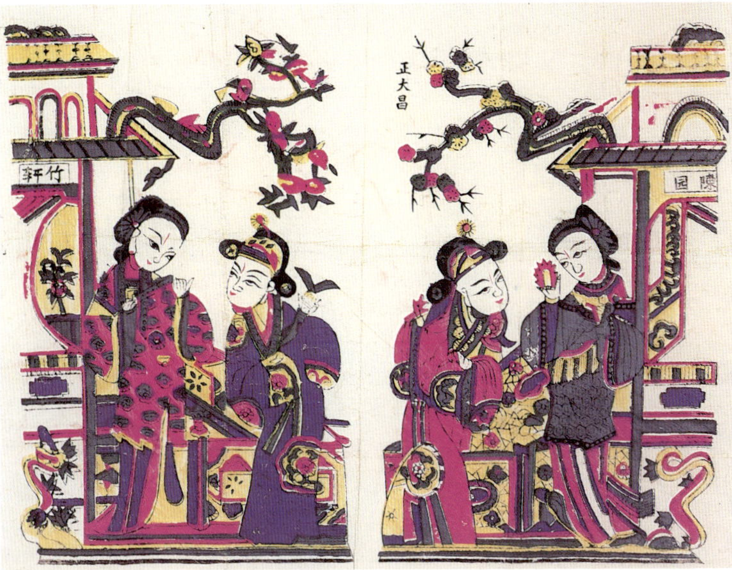

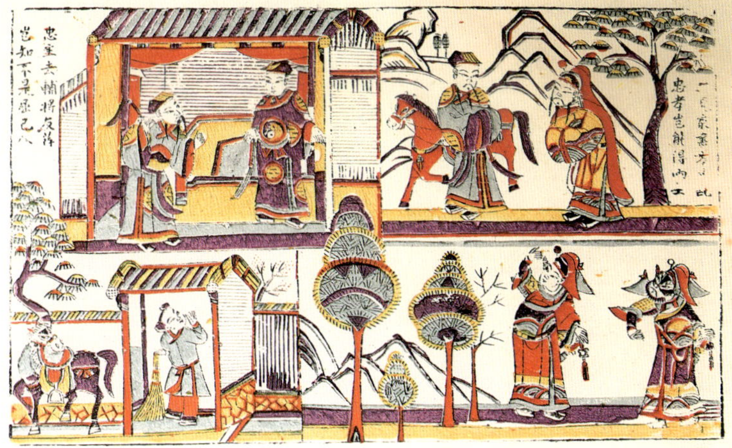

Top: Scenes from the opera *Pearl Tower* (door-picture), Tantou, Chunan, Henan
Bottom: Making Three Visits at the Thatched Cottage, a scene from the opera *Three Kingdoms*, Henan

long time they were used in ancestor worship or as a means to repel evil while welcoming goodness. Even in contemporary society, the understanding of the role of gods and immortals is widely accepted, and such images are still in great demand as a means to express one's wishes for a better, happier life.

Novels and operas

New Year Paintings depicting famous characters from Chinese literature or operatic traditions were originally derived from popular myths and legends, historical stories, folklore, novels, or popular operas. Famous stage setups or commonly known background images were used in the composition of New Year paintings. Famous novels and stories featured included such classic Chinese literary masterpieces as *A Dream of Red Mansions; Outlaws of the Marsh; Journey to the West; Three Kingdoms; Creation of the Gods*; *Romance of the Sui and Tang Dynasties*; *Yang Family Generals*; *Romance of the Cowherd and the Weaving Girl*; *The Legend of White Snake*; *General Yu e's Saga*; and *Romance of the Western Chamber.*

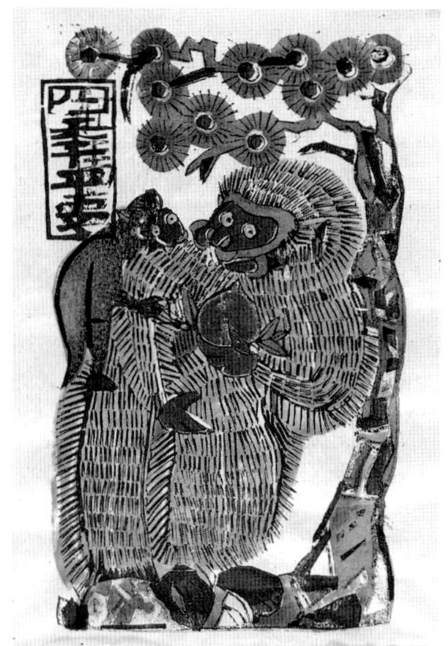

Peace in Four Seasons,
Fufeng, Shaanxi

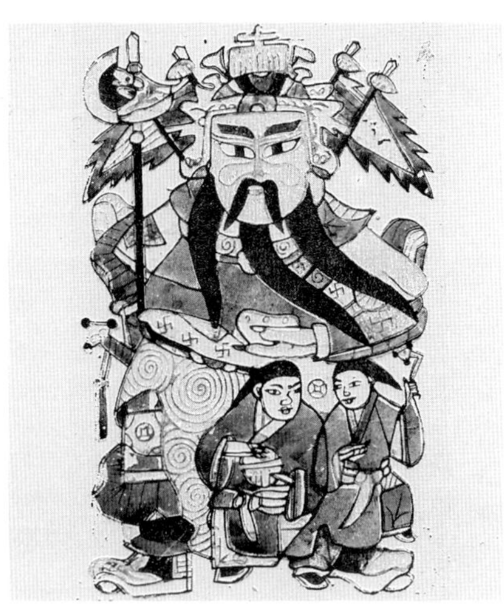

Door-god, Jiajiang, Sichuan

In the late Qing, novels and opera stories became very popular among the people, so paintings about these stories became an important part of New Year paintings since they were able to function as picture-stories as well as serial (or sequential) pictures. These themes were praised high moral standards, justice, and the banishment of evil. The characters in most of the paintings were almost always depicted in their stage costumes or the best way they could be instantly recognized by readers or viewers. The ones cherished most by the people were: *Weishui River, Beat the Noble Lady, The Stratagem of Empty City, Steal Fairy Weed, Family of General Yang, Lotus Lantern, Romance of the Western Chamber, Lake Boat, Fisherman's Revenge, Journey to the West* and *Twenty-four Examples of Filial Piety.*

Folk customs and lifestyle

During the Song Dynasty there were many paintings which depicted folk customs and festivals, such as the New Year, Lantern Festival, Dragon Boat Festival, and the Mid-Autumn Festival. The topic of everyday life was also a topic for paintings, such as farming, weaving, fishing, firewood collecting, and harvest time. New Year paint-

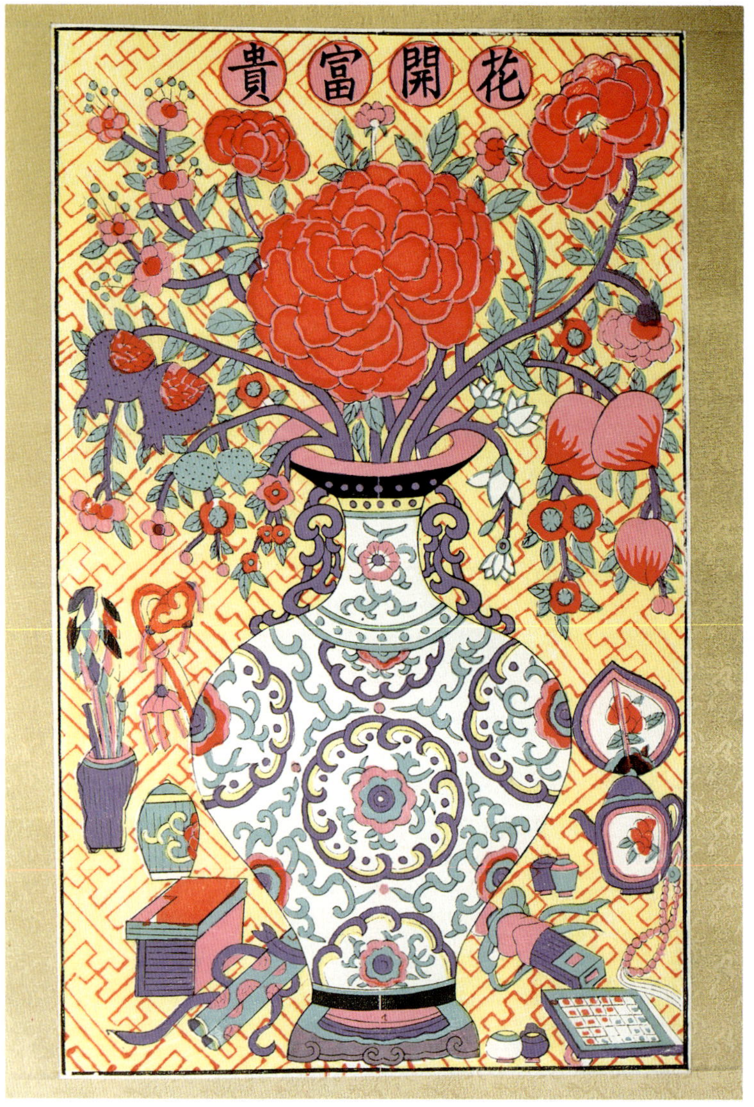

The Flower Blosson Brings Rich and Honor, Suzhou

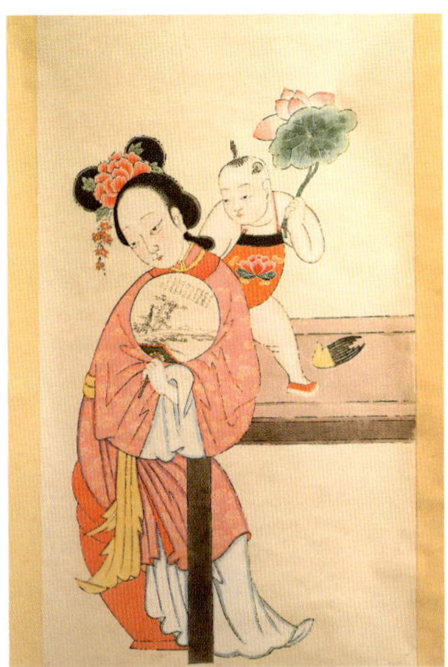

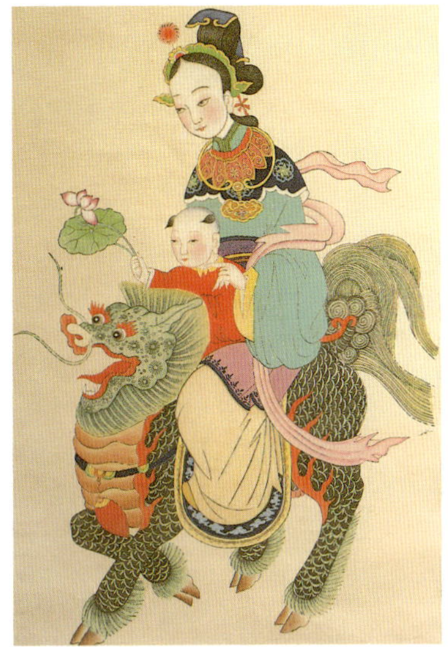

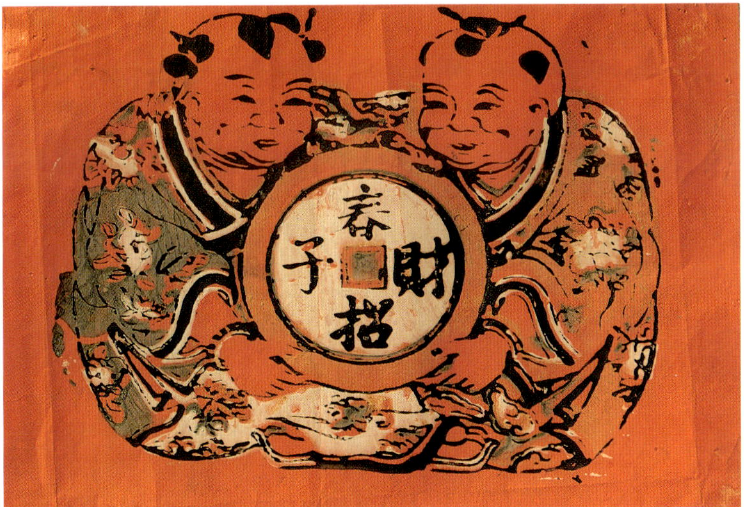

Top left: Having More Babies (letter paper), Houma, Shanxi
Top right: Qilin Delivering the Child (letter paper), Xinjiang, Shanxi
Bottom: Two Immortals, Zhangzhou, Fujian

ings also illustrated pictures of social activities, such as street and village life and the occupations of various craftspeople. Also reflected were political affairs, such as resistance against imperialism; as well as humor and social satire. The paintings reflected the feelings of folk painters and the experiences in their lives.

Auspicious scenes and creatures

These included the aforementioned tiger, deer, lion, crane, magpie, dragon, phoenix, Qilin (a mythical Chinese creature), carp, and other auspicious beasts and birds; flowers included the camellia, yulan magnolia, peony, lotus flower, chrysanthemum, and plum blossom, among others. Fruits and vegetables were also depicted, including pomegranate, fingered citron, bottle gourd, orange, and peach. There were also ancient auspicious objects and patterns of flowers and birds, such as the design of a flower vase with the characters of good fortune and longevity. Pictures of happy children and attractive young women were also examples of auspiciousness. New Year paintings of auspicious themes pleased people's satisfaction of longing for good fortune and dispelling evil.

Scenery and landscapes were other topics to be painted, and were also very popular among the people. These included places of interest, such as historical sites and famous mountains. Scenes of four seasons were often dotted with people engaged in traditional activities.

Miscellaneous paintings

The genre of folk painting reflected the everyday life of the people, including farming, harvesting, festival celebrations, and auspicious blessing. Some examples of this include the works, *Ten Busy Things of Men, Ten Busy Things of Women, Happy Life of Fishermen*, and *Nine Trades*. By the end of Qing Dynasty, there appeared many New Year paintings commenting on current affairs, depicting folk customs, and telling humorous or satirical stories, for example, *Marriage of the Mouse's Daughter, Monkey Robs Straw-hat*, and *Ten New Interesting Things*.

The genre of folk painting also includes forms of lantern painting, window painting paper, table-drape prints, wallpaper, painting on cloth, flower-bird characters, wood-block illustrations, and porcelain painting. Lantern painting, for example, was used to make lanterns for festive occasions, window painting paper was used to paste over window openings (in the days before glass was used as a window covering). Table-drape prints and wallpaper used to be pasted on cupboards or storage areas and on the sides of tables.

Cloth paintings were usually done sequentially, and would be displayed in the street for people to enjoy during the period which was from one week before the New Year Day to the middle of the first lunar month or the second day of the second lunar month.

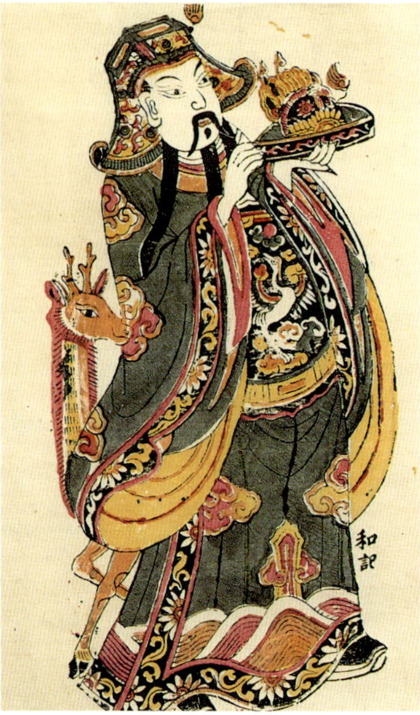

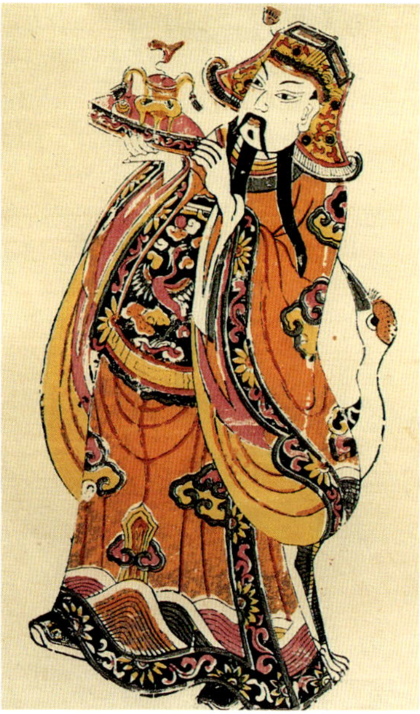

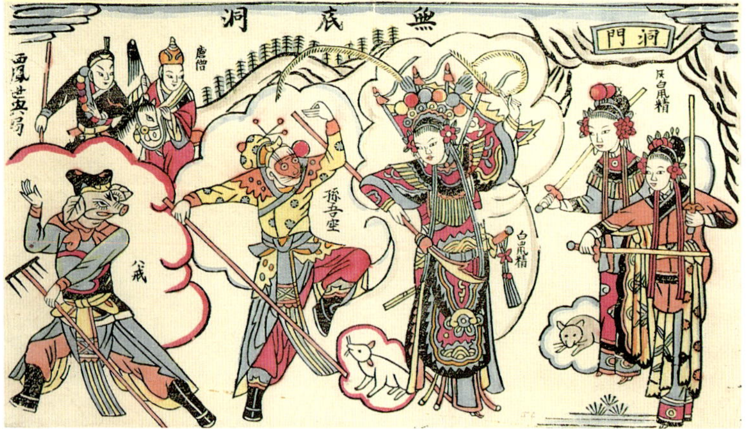

Top left: Six Harmoniousness as Spring, Shaanxi
Top right: Six Harmoniousness as Spring, Shaanxi
Botttom: Bottomless Cave, a scene from the opera *Journey to the West,* Shaanxi

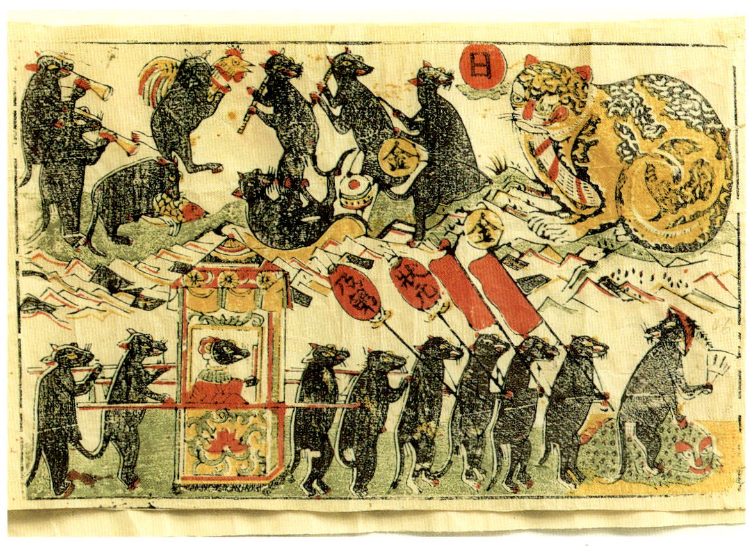

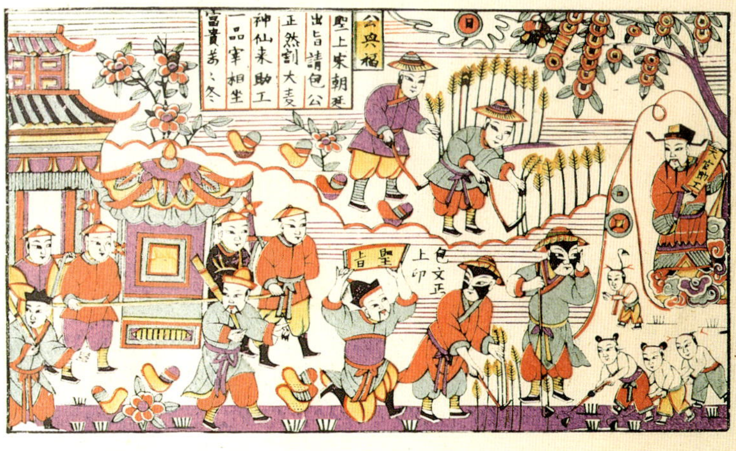

Top: Marriage of Mouse's Daughter, Zhangzhou, Fujian
Bottom: Heavenly Blessing, Henan

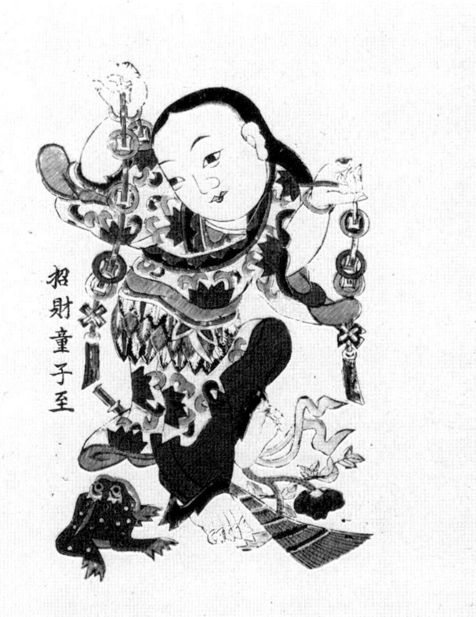

Liuhai Plays with Golden Turtle, Weixian, Shandong

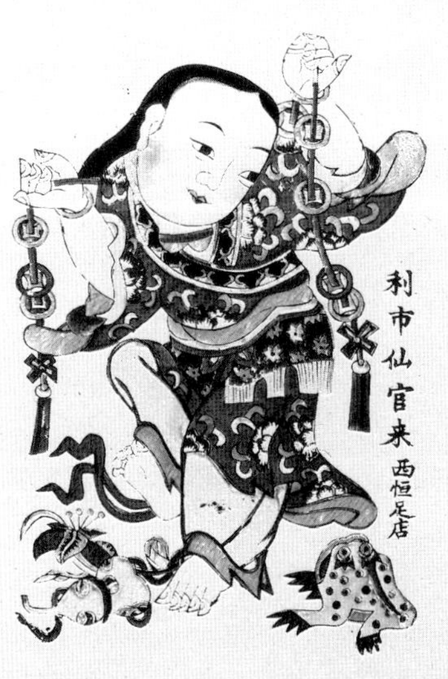

Liuhai Plays with Golden Turtle, Weixian, Shandong

Eight Immortals Playing Phoenix Chess, Weixian, Shandong

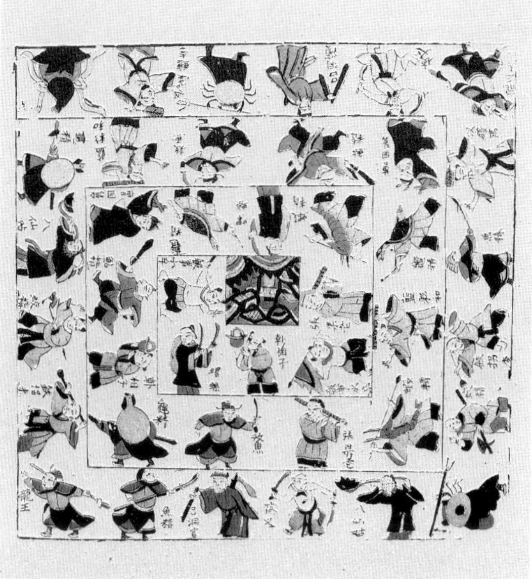

3. Main Production Areas of New Year Paintings

In China, the production of New Year paintings spread across the country, and each area has its own production base and its own distinct style. The production bases can be categorized into the following geographical regions:

Beijing, Tianjin and Hebei

New Year paintings in Beijing were mostly in the form of gods, immortals, Buddhist images, Paper Horse, and Door-God posters. Images of gods or Buddhist images were comparatively small in size and either printed by wood-block method or hand drawn. Some Door-God posters were as tall as three feet, with full composition printed in red, yellow, blue, and green. Some door paintings and lantern paintings were hand drawn. The Yangliuqing workshop was the

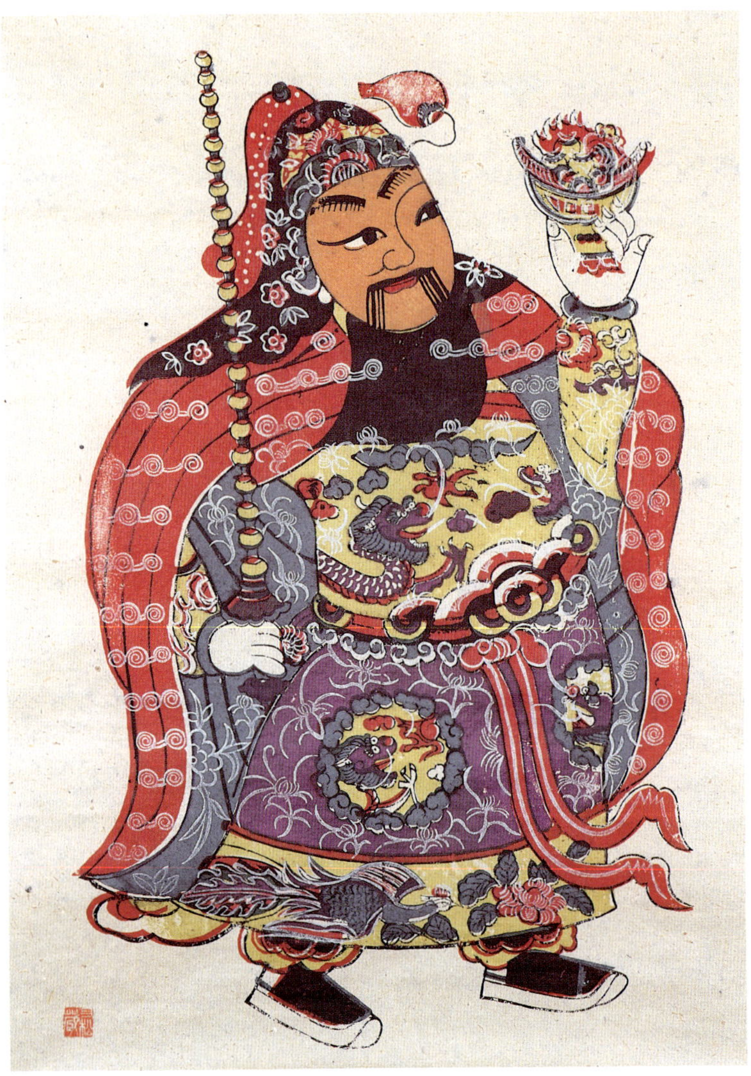

Heavenly Blessing (door poster), Jiangsu

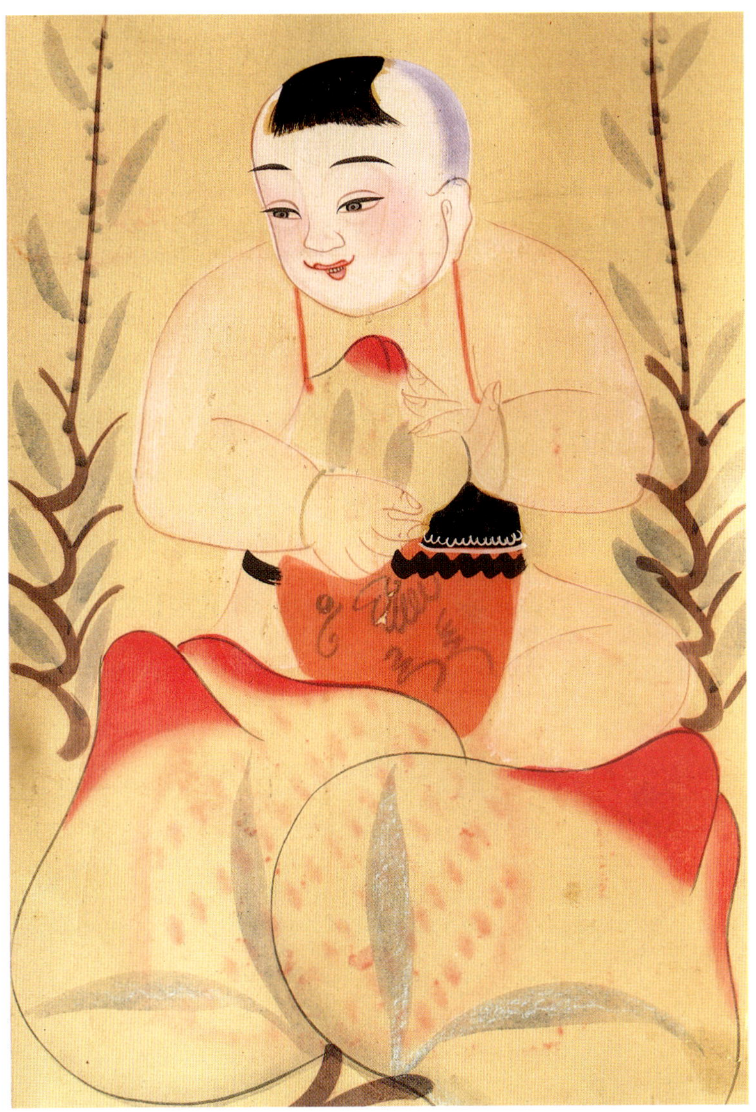

Picking Peaches, Gaomi, Shandong

center of production of New Year paintings in Tianjin, a tradition begun during the reign of Ming Emperor Wanli (1573-1619). Continuing to prosper during the Qing Dynasty, Yangliuqing could also output a large quantity of New Year paintings which were printed exquisitely in watercolor, and combined the techniques of wood-block printing and the "Gongbi" style of hand drawing. There were also paintings done in a free and unrestrained style. Their themes were broad, including folk life, historical stories, opera characters, children, beauties, flowers, landscape, gods, and current events. Some paintings could be as wide as 15 feet or more. Many such products were sold to Inner Mongolia, Xinjiang, Northeast China, Shandong and Northern China.

New Year paintings of Hebei were mainly produced in Wuqiang, Handan and Daming, with Wuqiang as the best known and most prosperous during the reign of Qing Emperor Jiaqing (1796-1820). The main themes of Wuqiang included opera stories, and riddles drawn on painted lanterns. Wujiang New Year paintings were mainly printed in red, yellow and green colors, in a bold, simple, and bright style.

Shaanxi and Shanxi

Hanzhong, Fengxiang, Shenmu, Pucheng and Chang'an were the production centers of New Year paintings in Shaanxi Province. Fengxiang, in particular, was perhaps the most famous for its New Year paintings which first appeared in the Ming Dynasty. Fengxiang's New Year paintings were mainly produced in South Xiaoli, North Xiaoli and Chen township in the western part of the city. Shaanxi was famous for its Door-God posters, with many varieties, Fengxiang alone having more than forty different types. In addition, other themes were represented, such as various folk customs, opera stories, myths and legends, and children.

Most of the New Year paintings produced at Hanzhong were also door posters, with many varieties including characters in novels and folk tales. Shaanxi has had a long tradition of culture, and New Year paintings have been influenced by other folk arts of the region. For instance, Door-God posters borrowed actors ' face painting from local operas. New Year paintings of Shaanxi were also sold to other provinces such as Gansu, Sichuan, Yunnan, Tibet, and Ningxia.

The New Year paintings of Shanxi were divided into two branches: northern and southern. The northern branch included Datong and Yinxian, and mainly produced window pictures with opera stories as their main theme. In the early period, these were printed only in black and white, while color wood-block printing was used later. The southern branch originated at Linfen, and later expended to Hongdong, Zhaocheng, Xiangfen, Qu'ao, Jishan, Houma, Xinjiang, and Hejin during the reigns of Qing Emperors Daoguang and Xianfeng (1821-1861), and lasting into the early years of the Republic after the Revolution of 1911. The main products of the southern branch were Door-God posters, Paper Horse pictures, imperial letter paper, couplets, paintings for large halls, dust-cleaning paper, and lantern paintings. Among these, the dust-cleaning paper and lantern paintings were some of the most artistic, half printed and half painted in five colors: red, pink, yellow, green, and black, with strong contrasts and bold, bright styles.

Shandong and Henan

Shandong featured many production centers of New Year paintings, and could be divided into two branches: eastern and western. Its eastern branch included Yangjiabu Township of Weixian County, Gaomi, and Pingdu. Its western branch included Liaocheng, Yanggu, Guanxian, old Shouzhang, and old Tangyi. Yangjiabu started to produce New Year paintings during the mid to late Ming Dynasty, and its workshops expanded to over a hundred during the late Qing. Yangjiabu New Year paintings featured many varieties such as Door-Gods, immortals, children, and opera characters.

Multiple wood-block techniques were used for color printing, plus adding rose color to the cheeks of the portraits which were done by hand. New Year paintings produced in Weixian were sold to Jiangsu, Anhui, Henan, Hebei, Inner Mongolia and the Northeast. Influenced by Weixian, nearby towns such as Gaomi and Pingdu also began to produce New Year paintings. Gaomi in particular thrived in producing paintings during the reign of Qing Emperor Guangxu (1975-1908), and its workshops spread to over 30 nearby villages.

The full-size paintings undertaken at Gaomi were the most famous, half-printed and half-painted. The watercolor full-size paintings were known as one of the "Three Excellences" of Gaomi. Pink and green were the main colors used, plus gold for added fine detail. Pingdu painting began during the reign of Qing Emperor Guangxu, and its style and variety were similar to Yangjiabu New Year paintings. Dongchang (today 's Weixian) New Year painting represented the western branch and originated in the Zhangqiu Township of old Shouzhang County. It was said that the art was introduced into the area from southern Shanxi during the Yuan Dynasty. The Dongchang workshop had become very prosperous by the end of the Qing Dynasty and the beginning of the Republic. Dongchang products were also sold to Shanxi, Henan, Hebei, and throughout the Northeast. New Year paintings produced in this area mainly featured Door-Gods, supernatural characters, and scenes and characters from various historical novels.

The production centers of New Year paintings in Henan were located mainly in the area of Kaifeng, Lingbao, Zhengzhou, Shangqiu, Luoyang, Zhoukou, Songxian, Zhengyang, Runan, Huojia and Xinxiang. In particular, the pictures produced by Zhuxian Township

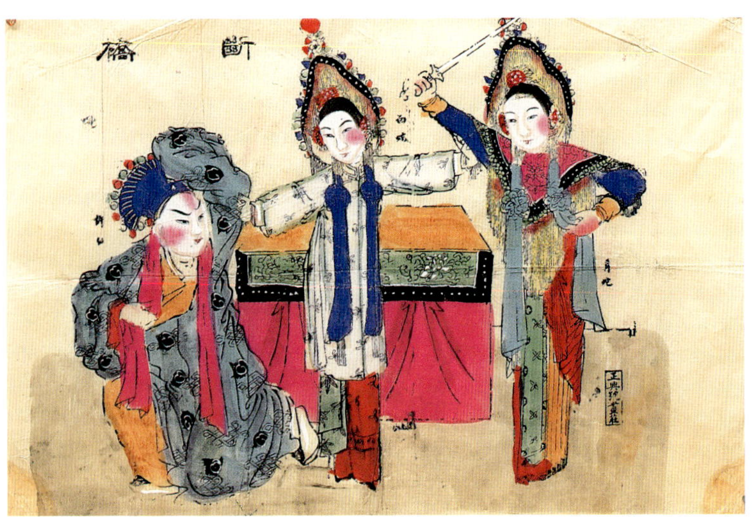

A Broken Bridge, a scene from the opera *White Snake*, Yangliuqing, Tianjin

Qilin Delivering the Child, Zhuxian Town, Kaifeng, Henan

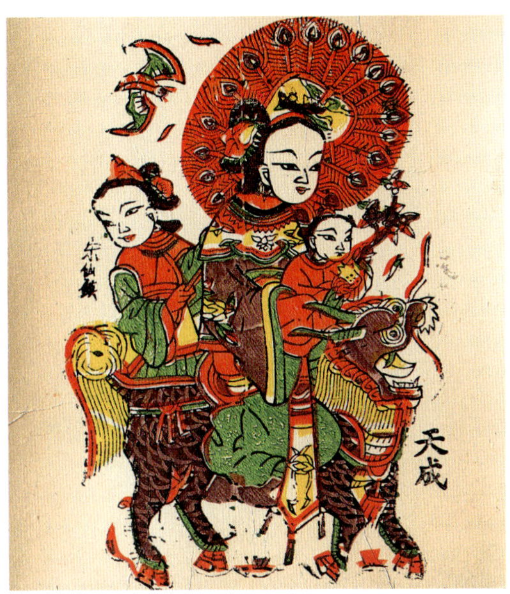

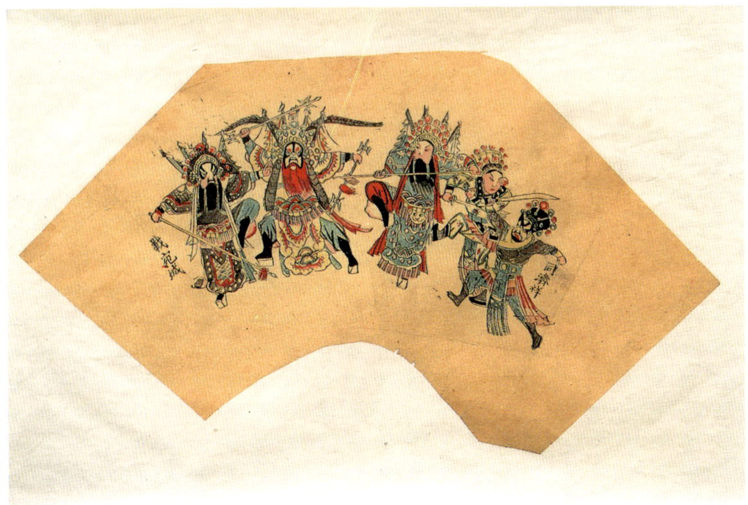

Fighting for Wancheng City, a scene from Peking Opera *Three Kingdoms*, (fan spread), Xinxian, Shandong

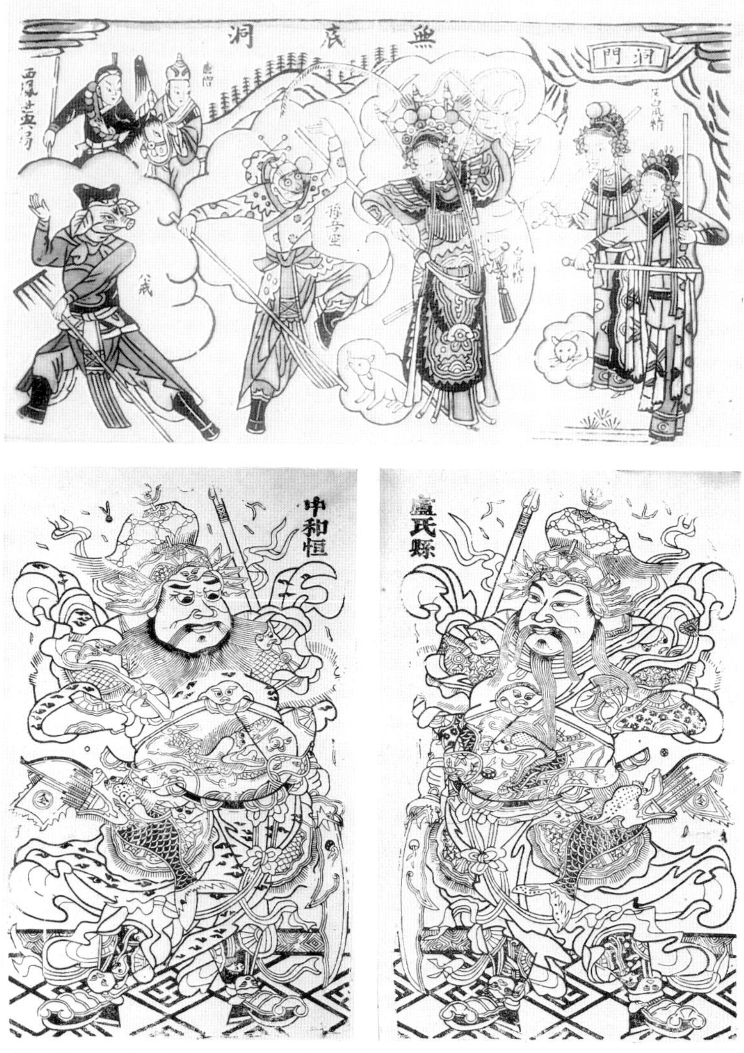

Top: Bottomless Cave, a scene from classical novel *Journey to the West*, Shaanxi
Bottom left: A Warrior Door-god, Henan
Bottom right: A Warrior Door-god, Henan

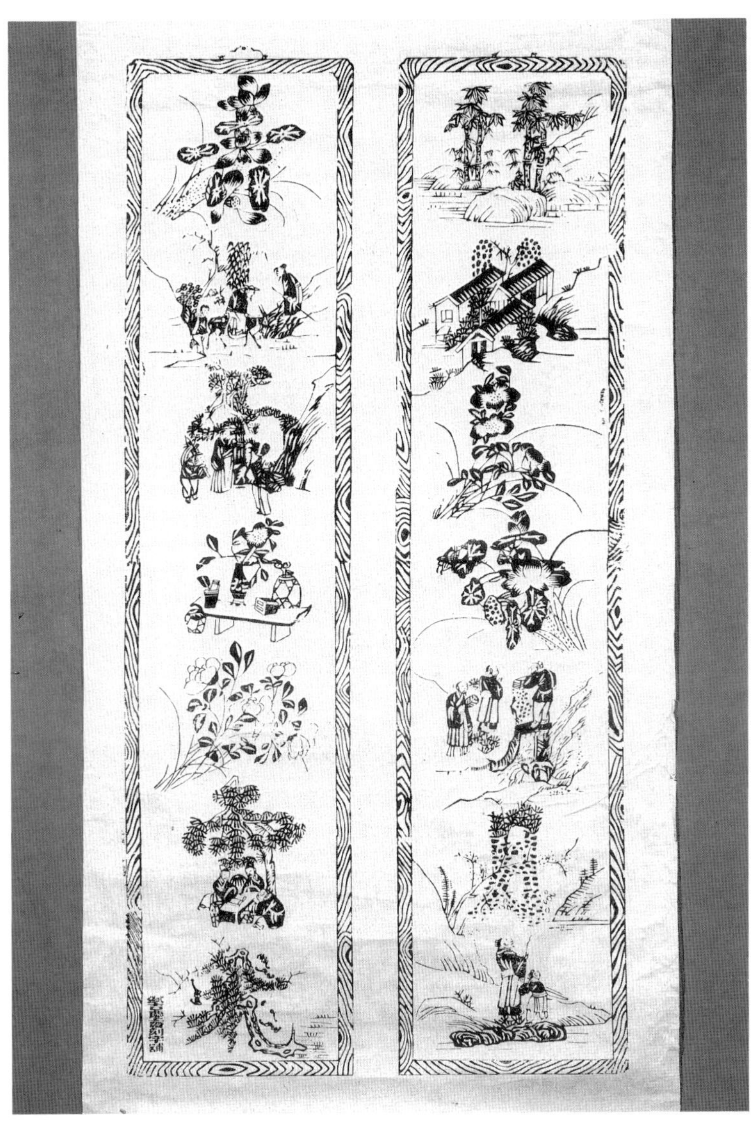

Antithetical couplet, Wuqiang, Hebei

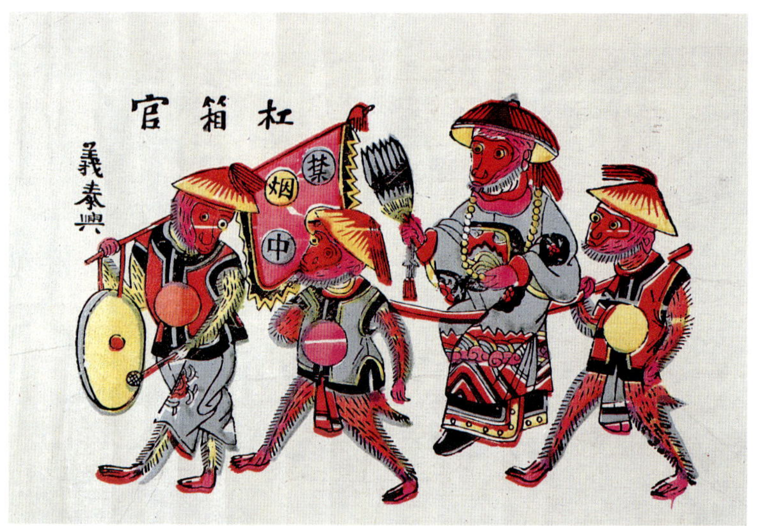

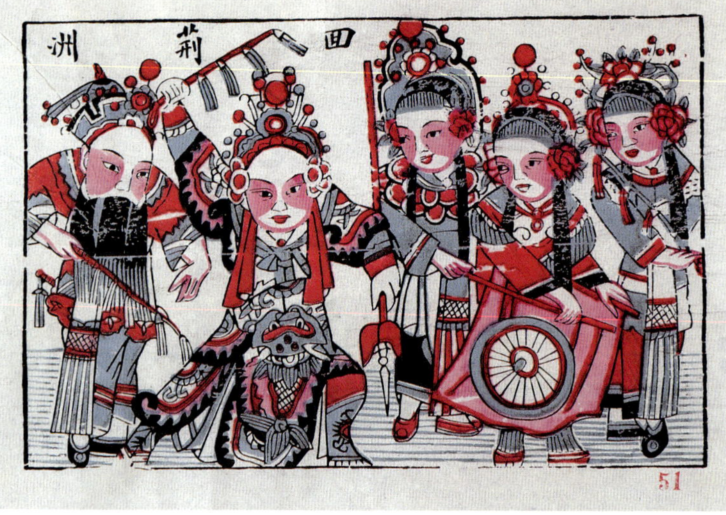

Top: Carrying Confiscated Opium, Wuqiang, Hebei
Bottom: Back to Jingzhou, a scence from the Wawa opera *Three Kingdoms*, Wuqiang, Hebei

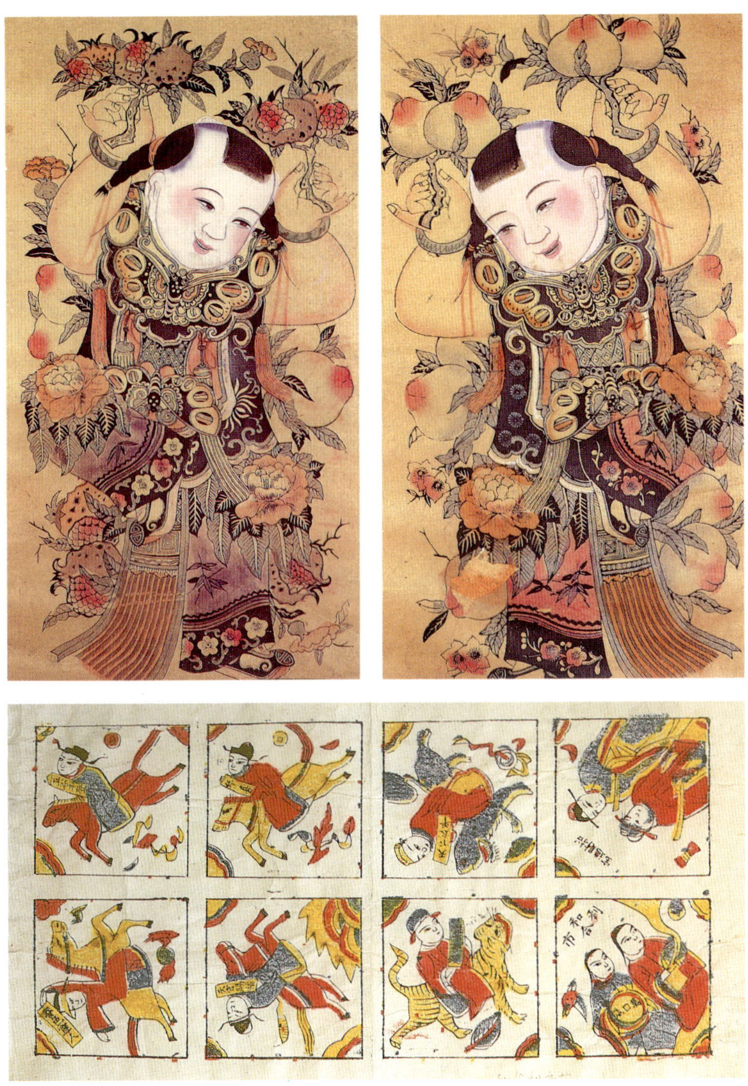

Top left: More Happiness and Long Life, Gaomi, Shandong
Top right: More Happiness and Long Life, Gaomi, Shandong
Bottom: Good Fortune, Henan

(near Kaifeng), whose origins could be traced back to Northern Song Dynasty, flourished during the Qing. Popular themes included opera stories and characters. Orange, dark green and bright yellow were the main colors used by the Zhuxian artisans. All the paintings were wood-block prints done in color, without any retouching by hand. The lines were thick and rich in color and the style was simple and traditional. Zhuxian' s portrait paintings also had a unique style: there was a curve and an orange coloring along the eyebrows.

Jiangsu and Zhejiang

There were many places in Jiangsu Province producing New Year paintings, including: Suzhou, Nanjing, Wuhu, Yangzhou, Xuzhou, Dongtai, and Nantong. The Taohuawu area near Suzhou was one of the largest, originating during the Ming Dynasty and flourishing during the Qing Dynasty at the time of the reigns of Emperors Yongzheng and Qianlong (1723-1795). Most of the workshops were located in the Tiger Hill area, and utilized techniques from both hand drawing and wood-block printing. These paintings featured bright and elegant colors, mainly red, pink, yellow, green, and gray, and all displayed fine workmanship. In later development, Taohuawu paintings were also influenced by the technique of Western paintings. The paintings were sold in Jiangsu, Zhejiang, Anhui and Shandong and also exported to Southeast Asia. Taohuawu New Year paintings had made influence to different degrees to those produced in South China. Nantong New Year paintings were printed in red, purple, blue and green, and also printed with silver and golden lines on clothes. Its main products were supernatural horses and Door-Gods, liked very much by people in northern Jiangsu. Yangzhou paintings had many varieties, but were similar to those of Suzhou. Shanghai New Year paintings were started in the reign of Qing Emperor Guangxu (1875-1908), greatly influenced by Taohuawu integrating traditional lithography with Western painting techniques. Its calendar posters were very unique.

The production of Zhejiang New Year paintings was centered in Hangzhou and Yuhang, with Paper Horse and god images as their main products. Introduced from Suzhou and with some improvements, they were printed delicately in harmonious tones by two different kinds of wood-block plates: strong and light impressions. The strong one made special dots on the paintings.

Fujian and Taiwan

Quanzhou, Zhangzhou, Fuding and Fu'an were the main production areas of New Year paintings in Fujian. Quanzhou paintings, which flourished during the reign of Qing Emperor Qianlong, had enjoyed a close relationship with wood-block illustrations in books during the Yuan and Ming dynasties. These were mainly Door-God and Buddhist image posters and magic symbols, printed in yellow and green colors (sometimes adding blue and white), and black ink

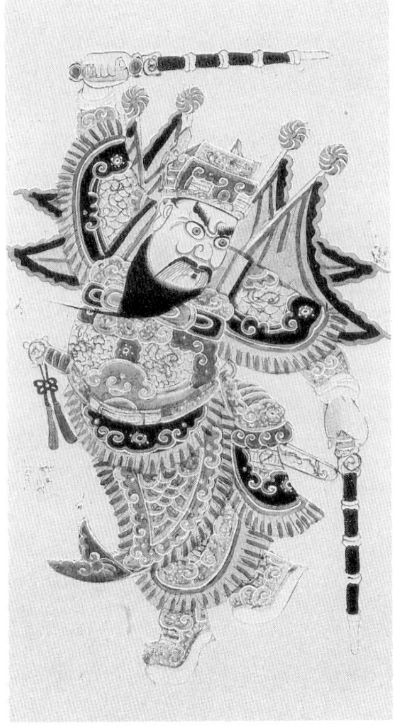

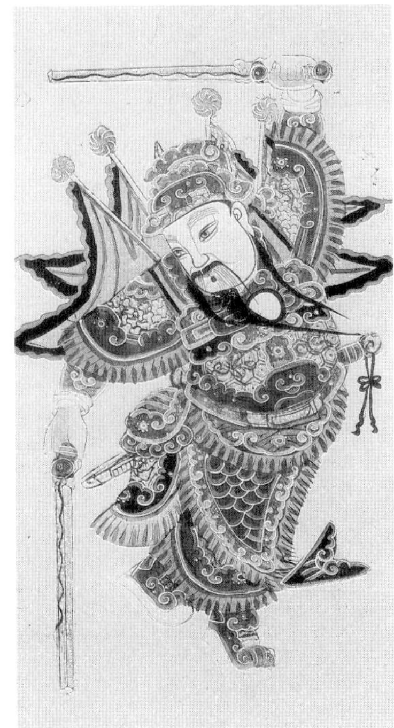

Top: Jingde (door-god), Jiangsu
Bottom: Qinqiong (door-god), Jiangsu

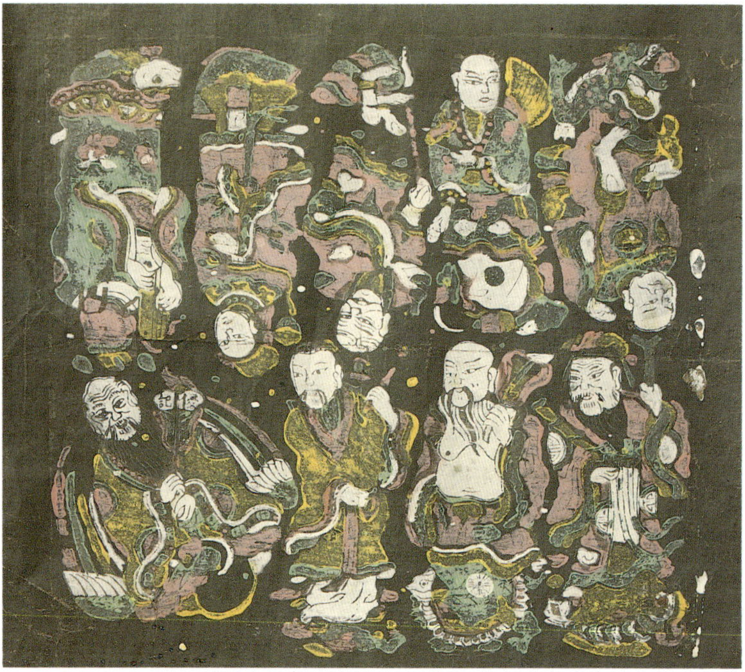

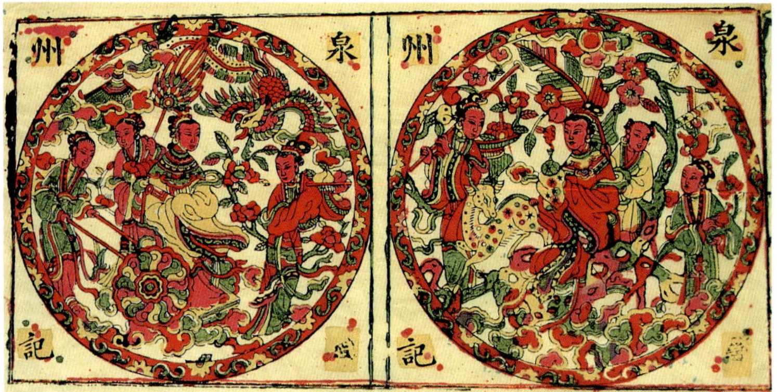

Top: Black Eight Immortals, Zhangzhou, Fujian
Bottom: Good Blessing, Quanzhou, Fujian

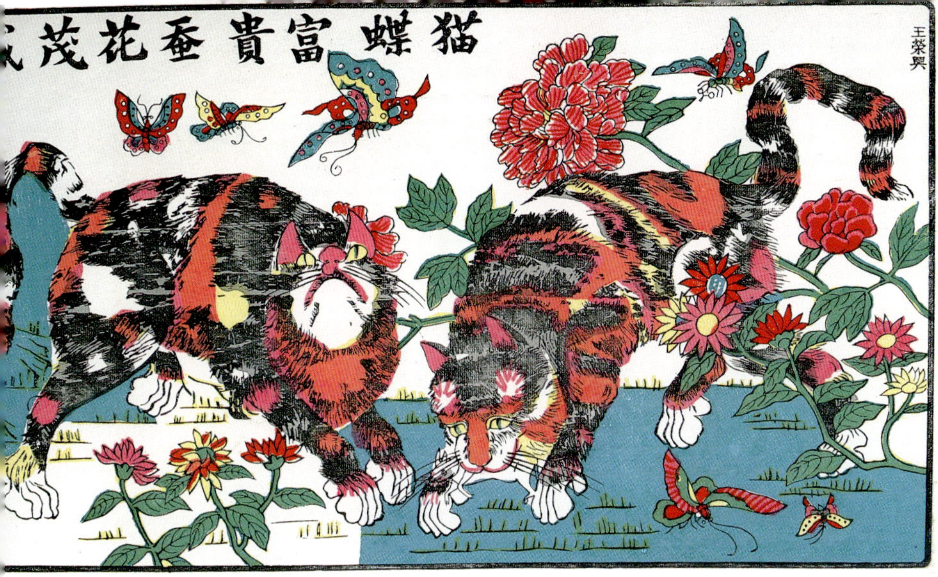

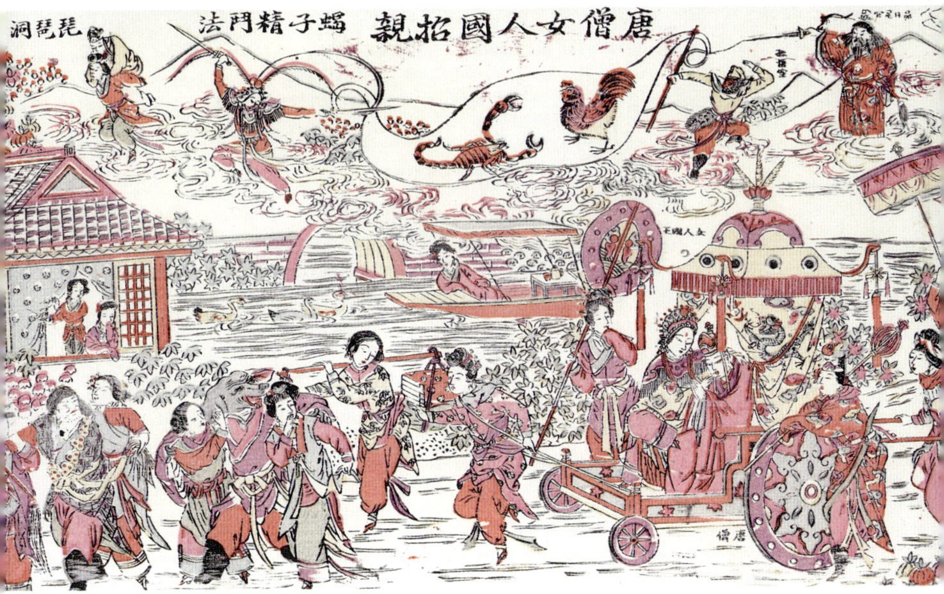

Top: Cats and Butterflies, symbolizing wealth and honor, Taohuawu, Suzhou
Bottom: Monk Xuanzang forced to marry in the Women Kingdom, a scene from the *Journey to the West*, Taohuawu, Suzhou

with wood-block plates on bamboo paper or red paper. Zhangzhou paintings started during the late Ming and early Qing. By the end of Qing, there were already 150 patterns, with door posters, lantern paintings, Buddhist offerings, and folk products as the main items produced. Its door posters often used red as a background, printed with light green, light yellow and light blue, and posted on the front doors of houses. Decorative New Year paintings were mostly printed in red, orange, and green with black lines on white paper. Another type of door posters was used on the gates of temples. They were in sets, four pictures in one set, and printed in light blue and red colors on a black background. The sets were composed of such subjects as the "four beasts" (elephant, lion, tiger, and leopard); the "four-season flowers" (peony, water lily, chrysanthemum, and plum blossom); and the "four Gods" (Fortune, Wealth, Longevity and Happiness). The regions of Fuding and Fu'an were close to Zhejiang, so the styles of the paintings produced there were different from those of Zhangzhou and Quanzhou. Fuding's square paintings with opera themes were unique—combining opera stories with beautiful painted faces. These were first printed with black ink lines and later painted in color by hand.

The island of Taiwan belonged to Fujian province before the time of Qing Emperor Guangxu (1875-1908), so New Year paintings were introduced there from Zhangzhou and Quanzhou. Production in Taiwan was centered in the southern part of the island, and the styles mainly depicted Door-Gods, Buddhist images, opera stories, and magic symbols. There were also "Eight Trigram Incantations," and lion heads which were used for decoration on boat cabin doors or on the sterns of boats.

Guangdong and Guangxi

Foshan, Xinhui, Anbu and Chenghai were the main production areas of New Year paintings in Guangdong. In the old days, most of the workshops of New Year paintings were located around Fulu Lane and Shuixiang Lane in Foshan. Images and posters of gods accounted for the biggest portion. Large posters were used for Taoist rites, while smaller ones were displayed during the New Year or used during worship. There were two kinds of paintings: one printed in color by wood-block and the other printed in black lines with drawings done by hand. Some pictures were printed on colored paper. The subjects included Door-Gods, opera stories, gods and dieties, and auspicious symbols. Anbu and Chenghai mainly produced Paper Horse pictures known as "southern gold," which symbolized wealth.

Guangxi New Year paintings were mainly produced in Guilin, Quanzhou, Nanning and Dongxing. Guilin paintings started during the reign of Qing Emperor Qianlong and were continually improved. Red and blue were the two primary colors with a little yellow, following a very traditional approach. Quanzhou was famous for horse pictures. Nanning mainly produced Door-God posters and posters of children. One well-known design was to depict small children on a yellow background, which were used by minority ethnic groups. Dongxing was a residence of the Jing ethnic minority, and the New Year paintings produced there were printed with the signs or characters symbolizing wealth, longevity, and auspiciousness.

Sichuan, Guizhou and Yunnan

The main production centers of New Year paintings in Sichuan were located in Mianzhu, Jiajiang, Liangping, Chengdu, and Jianyang, among which Mianzhu was the biggest. Beginning to develop at the end of Ming Dynasty and the beginning of Qing Dynasty, Mianzhu paintings could be divided into two main categories: red and black. For the red category, black ink lines were printed first, then the picture was drawn in by hand. These were small in size. For the black category, rubbings were made in red and black colors of famous works of calligraphy and painting. Different techniques of carving and painting were used to depict different styles. The products were sold to Yunnan, Guizhou, Qinghai, Tibet, Xinjiang, Anhui, Hunan and Hubei, and even to India, Burma, Vietnam, and other countries with Chinese communities. New Year paintings of Jiajiang used timber red, camphor red, Japanese pagoda tree yellow, and fustic green from minerals and plants. The colors looked extremely bright on cloudy or even rainy days. The Door-God posters were also known as "Yellow and Red Door-God" posters. New Year paintings of Jiajiang were locally referred to as "floral paper," a local bamboo paper printed by color wood blocks and using local dyes. They were mostly in small size and with natural

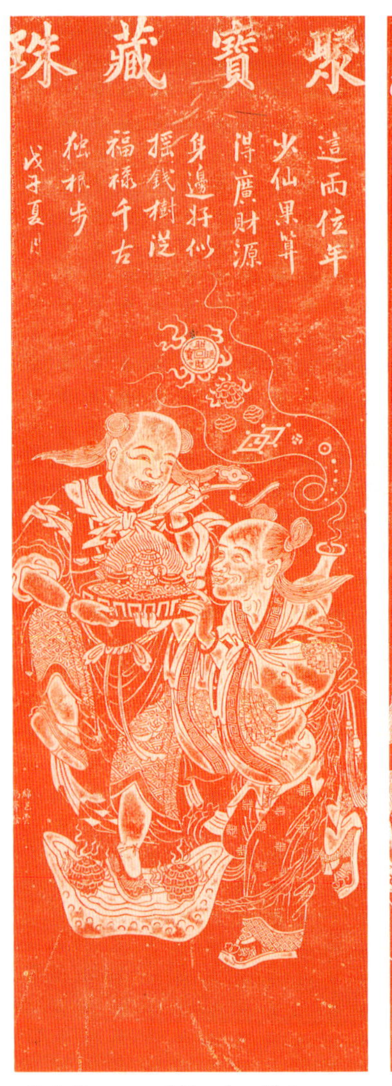

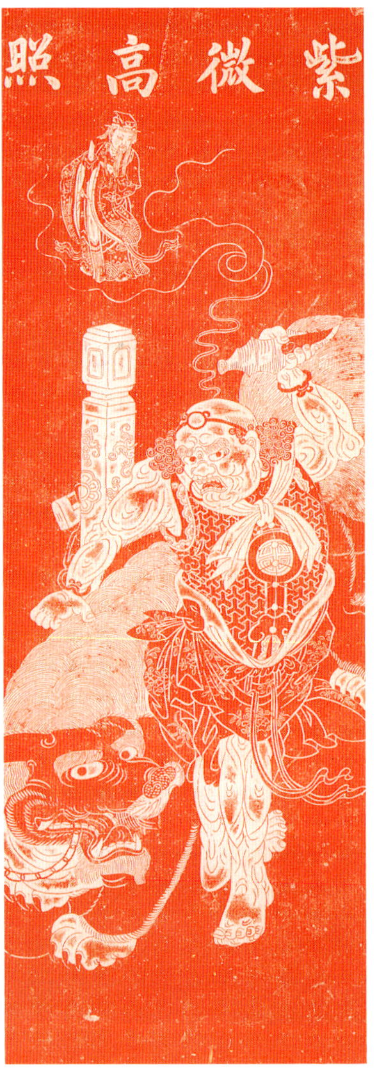

Left: Bonanza, Mianzhu, Sichuan
Right: Good Fortune, Mianzhu, Sichuan

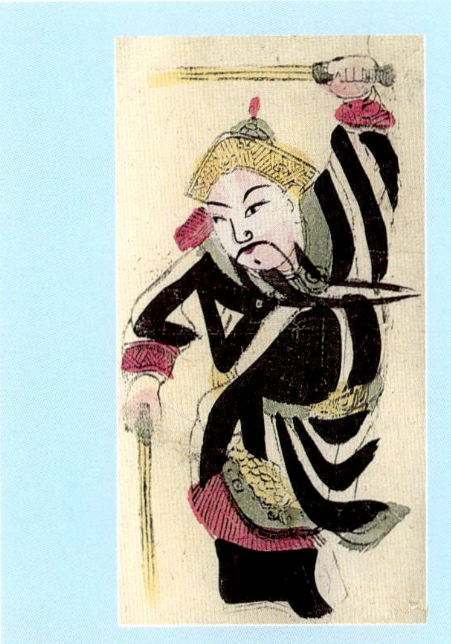

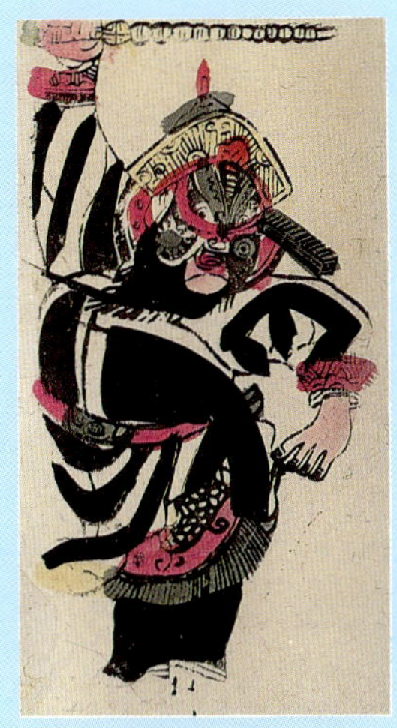

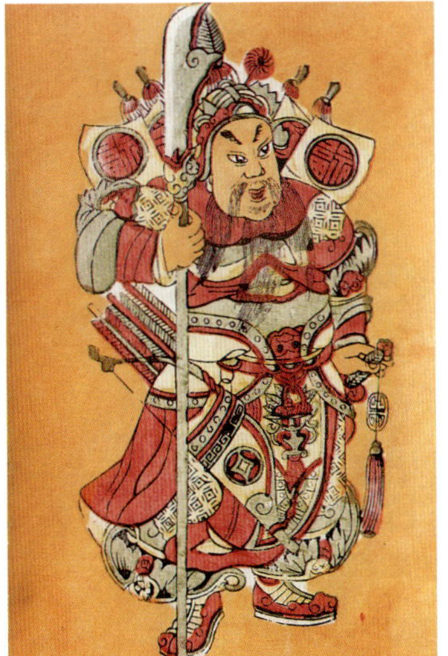

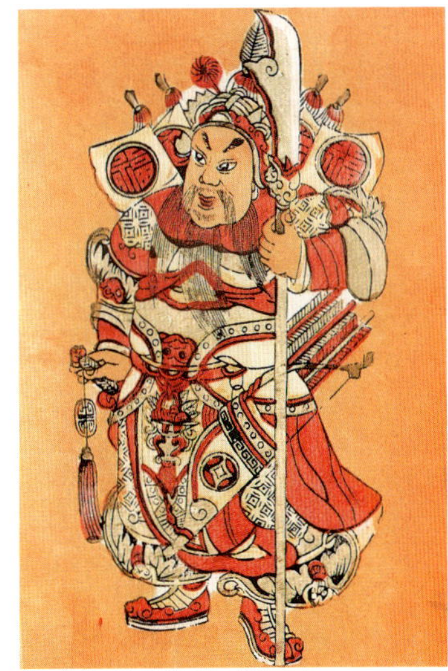

Top: Qinqiong and Jinde (door-gods), Chunan, Hunan
Bottom left: General Holding a Sword (door-picture), Foshan, Guangdong
Bottom right: General Holding a Sword (door-picture), Foshan, Guangdong

and bold styles. Liangping New Year paintings were mainly produced in Pingjin and Yuanze. The locals not only printed posters but also produced paper. They combined printing with painting for the New Year, mostly in the production of Door-God posters. Ranping specialized in "floral paper", pasted horizontally over doors, with depictions of opera stories. Guizhou New Year paintings were produced at Anshun.

New Year paintings of Yunnan were produced mainly in Baoshan, Lijiang, Nanjian and Baqu. Most of the places are inhabited by minority ethnic groups. All used a bold style with the exception of those from Lijiang, which were more delicate and fine in terms of detail and workmanship. Baqu is the place where the Dai ethnic group lives. At their annual "Water Festival," banners, like New Year paintings, were proudly hung, displaying auspicious wishes using bright colors.

Hunan, Hubei and Anhui

Hunan New Year paintings were represented by Tantou Township, Longhui County. New Year painting was first introduced into Tantou from Sichuan and Guizhou, and then formed its own style. First, white color was brushed onto locally-made paper, then colors and ink lines were printed by using wood-block techniques, and finally rose-color retouching was made on the cheeks of the printed figures.

Hubei had many workshops making New Year paintings, such as Junxian, Xiaogan, Huangpi, and Wuhan. The themes were mainly flowers, birds, Door-Gods, and auspicious symbols. The styles were very traditional with rich colors. Most Hubei paintings were generally small in size.

Anhui New Year paintings were produced at Fuyang, Linquan, Boxian, Suxian, Jieshou, Wuhu, and Taihe. Paintings of Fuyang and Linquan were introduced from Zhuxian in Henan, while those of Wuhu were greatly influenced by Suzhou paintings.

Areas inhabited by minority ethnic groups also produced many New Year paintings. Baotou of Inner Mongolia produces pictures which were highly influenced by Beijing. The Mongol custom was to hang large-size "Duobao Jingge" (Treasure Painting) in their yurts, which featured such auspicious symbols as bells, tripods, flower vases, and bowls of fruit. Other forms of New Year paintings were posters printed with opera stories, and indigo-like paper parcels which were meant to be burned as offerings at religious ceremonies.

Xinjiang New Year paintings mainly depicted flowers, Western-style buildings and gardens. Most of the themes and styles were introduced from Tianjin.

In general, Tibet did not follow the custom of hanging New Year paintings, but print shops there produced Gods and deities, Paper Horse, auspicious symbols, and large banners.

4. Art and Technique of New Year Painting

New Year painting is an art form appreciated by both artists and everyday people. Not only did it share a common origin with a more formal, scholarly form of painting, but it also reflected the profound values of Chinese folk culture and aesthetics.

New Year paintings absorbed valuable artistic and thematic ele-

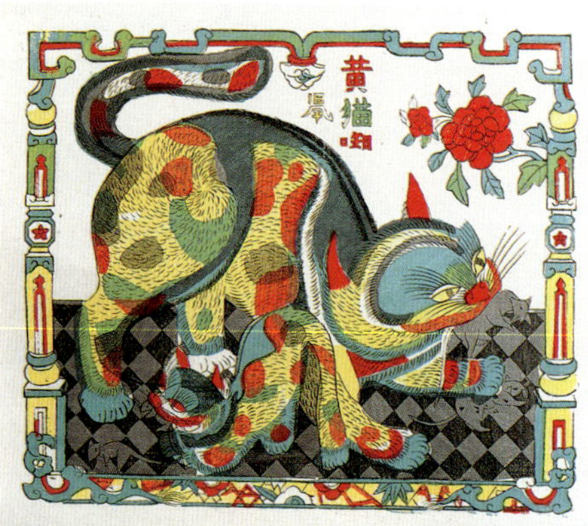

Yellow Cat Catching a Mouse, (door-picture), Taohuawu, Suzhou

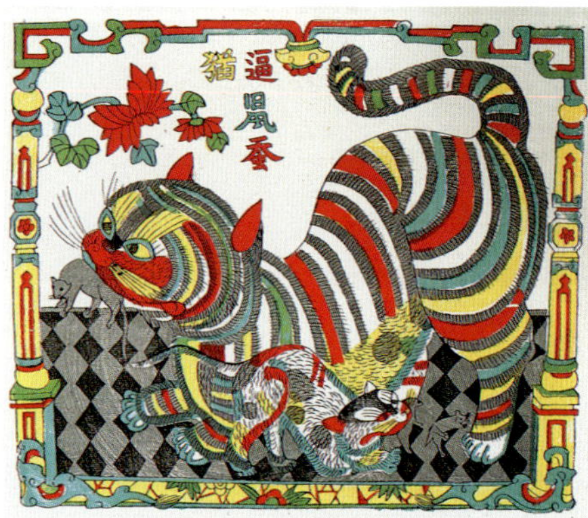

Cat Protecting Silkworm (door-picture), Taohuawu, Suzhou

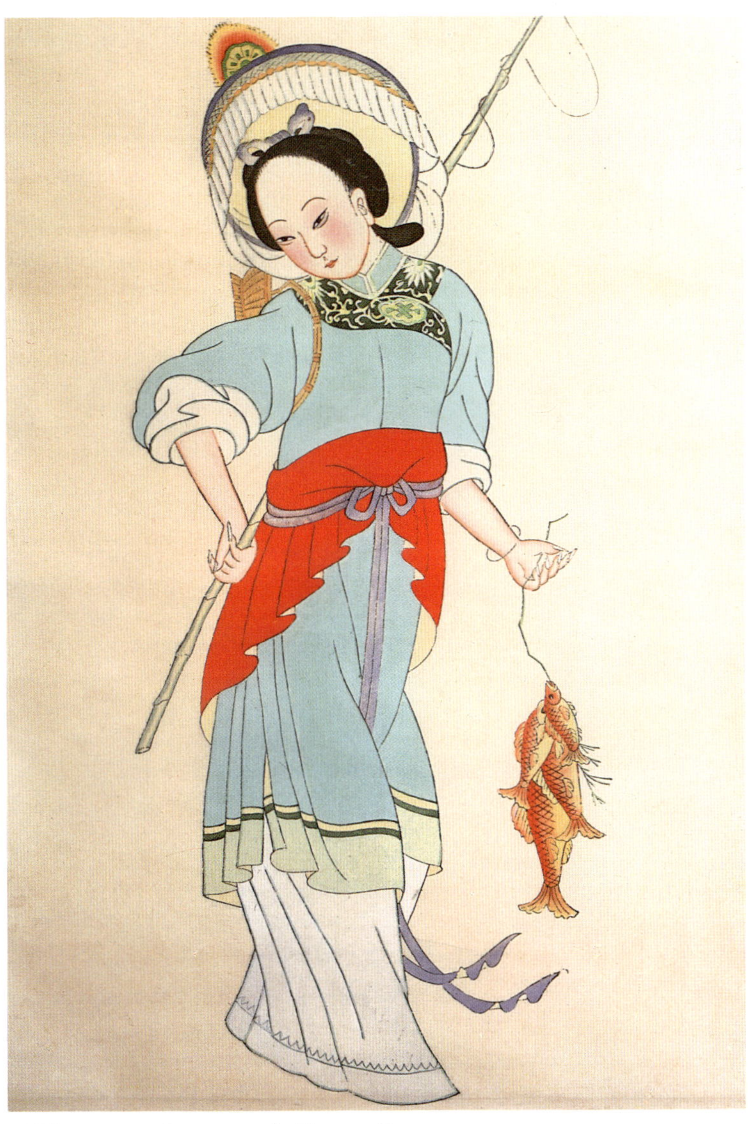

Fisherwoman (letter paper), Houma, Shanxi

ments from scholarly painting in terms of subject matter and technique. Formal painting, meanwhile, was influenced by many elements common to New Year Paintings. Thus, New Year paintings appealed to both "high" and "low" categories of art. In recent years, many professional painters have joined in the creation of New Year paintings, and new ideas and techniques were used.

Traditional folk artisans have also raised their own level by becoming more professional. New Year paintings have evolved from a pure folk art product to a type of medium with a higher aesthetic value, but remain closely related to popular art encountered in everyday life.

The concept and execution of New Year paintings represents the soul of the painter and his or her creation. New Year paintings were, at first, a response to nature, divination, and ancestor worship. Later, it evolved to encompass the wishes of the common people and their desire to attain prosperity while expelling evil.

Though these essential concepts had started to have relatively limited practical use in later centuries, much of the traditional Chinese ideas were still very much present. Throughout history, people wished for the continuation of their family line, and that their family members would enjoy long life and prosperity. The art forms of New Year paintings, their themes, images, compositions, painting and printing techniques, all are subject to the concept, function and aesthetics of the people.

The composition of New Year paintings successfully displays theme and content and also plays an important role in the decorative and festive functions of everyday Chinese society. The composition of New Year paintings is full and harmonious. This can be seen in all forms of New Year paintings, as well as in other folk arts of China, such as opera, fiction, and myths and legends. For instance, the main subject and subordinate subject are arranged in a particular order, with images of Gods, deities, and historical characters receiving large, often central placement. In some posters depicting farming and weaving, all people, animals, and scenery are placed accordingly, some big, some small, some at the center, some at the edges, some loosely arranged, and others densely packed, creating pictures of varying atmosphere. Large-size posters of landscapes and marketplaces are usually painted in the form of a bird 's-eye-view. In opera story posters, the characters, stage settings, and instruments, are arranged by using forced perspective and line-dot combinations. On Door-God posters, figures are usually arranged symmetrically, with rich colors, strong brush strokes, and unique layouts. But, these images also possess fine, delicate details.

The pursuit of aesthetic integrity and the perception of bounty, fullness, and perfection, can also be seen in the images of New Year paintings. Figures are drawn as if seen straight-on. Profiles are typically not used. Door-Gods are usually in static poses and fill out most of the picture; officials are usually seen as having a big belly; military officers are usually strong and stand at the ready. Other images follow a similar pattern, demonstrating the idea of perfection. Other auspicious animals, flowers, vegetables and fruits are presented in the same way.

Bright, rich colors are another feature of New Year paintings. Traditional folk culture and aesthetics of the people greatly influenced the use and matching of colors. The traditional presentation of "five-colors," the philosophical concepts, religious beliefs, ethics, and im-

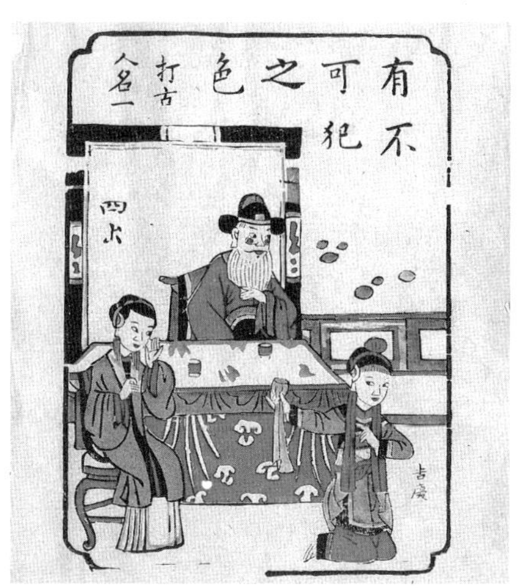

Riddle picture, Wuqiang, Hebei

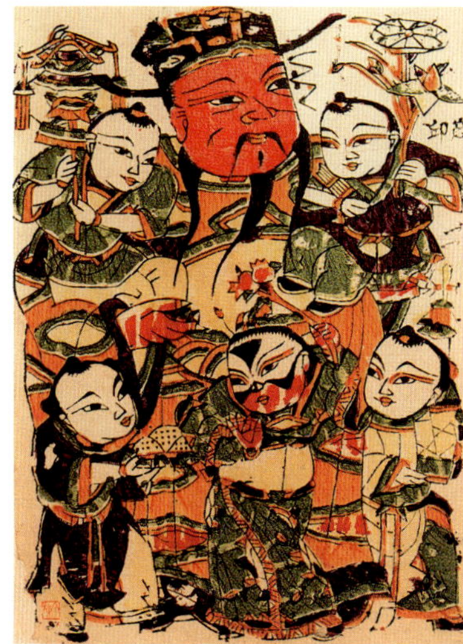

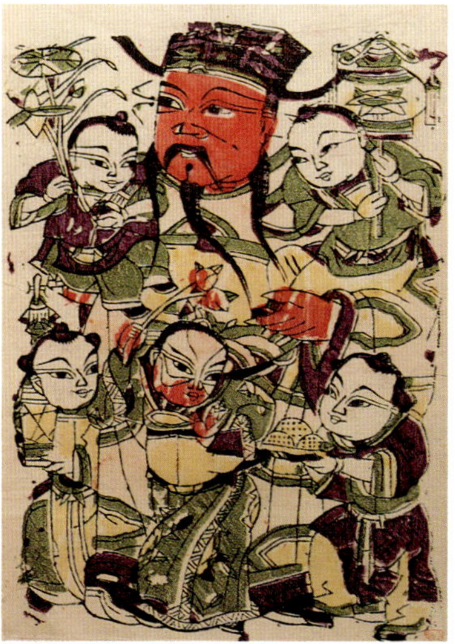

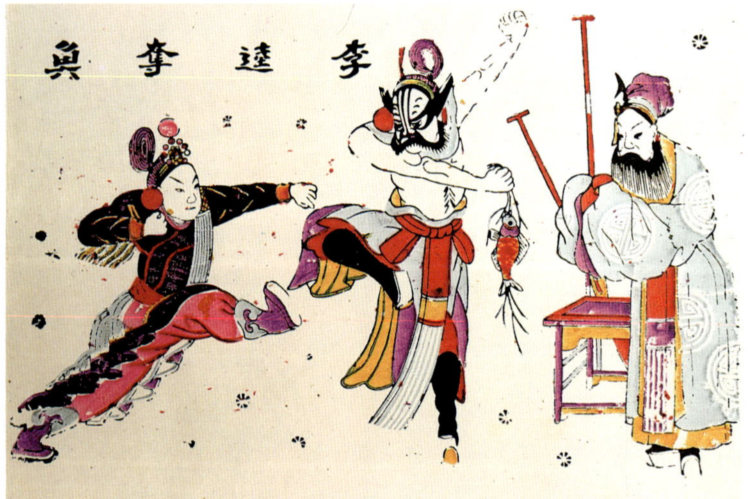

Top left: Wealth and Rank, Zhuxian Town, Kaifeng, Henan
Top right: Wealth and Rank, Zhuxian Town, Kaifeng, Henan
Bottom: Likui Snatching the Fish, a scene from the opera *Outlaws of the Marsh*, Shandong

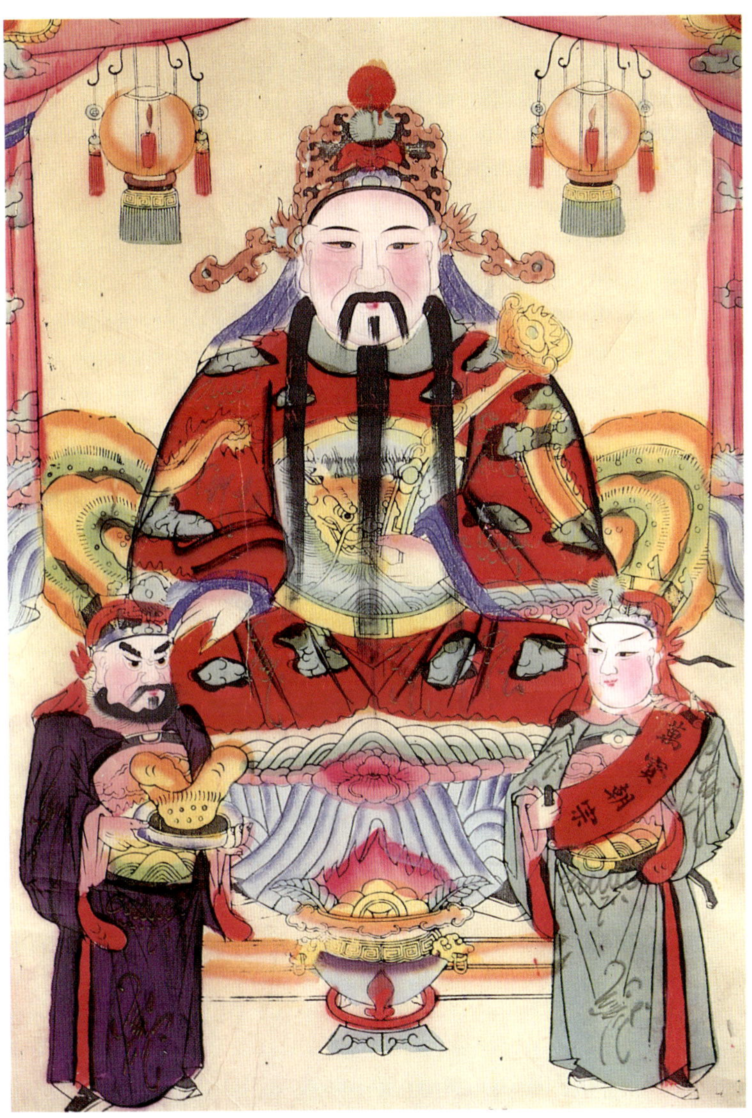

God of Wealth, Shandong

portance of family or clan tradition all have influences on the use of color.

Color also plays a profound role in the visual effect of the paintings, which may look fresh and bright. This is not surprising given the festive environment in which New Year paintings are typically displayed, but there are also some paintings created using delicate, light colors, such as light blue, light green, gray and golden hues, balanced with outlines of black ink. These paintings are simple and elegant. Yangliuqing New Year paintings, for example, are printed in light colors displaying elegant composition, but the clothes and faces of the characters are still in bright and rich colors to create a vivid and lively atmosphere. Another example is the small-size door poster produced in Fujian. It has black as a background, and is painted in rich colors, giving an effect of beautiful lacquer painting. No matter which color is used, the purpose is to show the spirit of the objects but not the

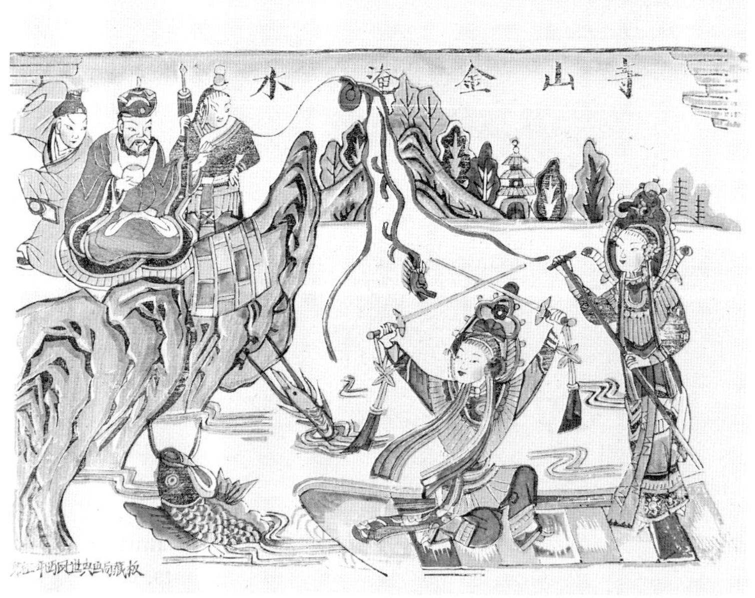

Water Submerging Golden Hill, a scene from the opera *White Snake*, Fengxiang, Shaanxi

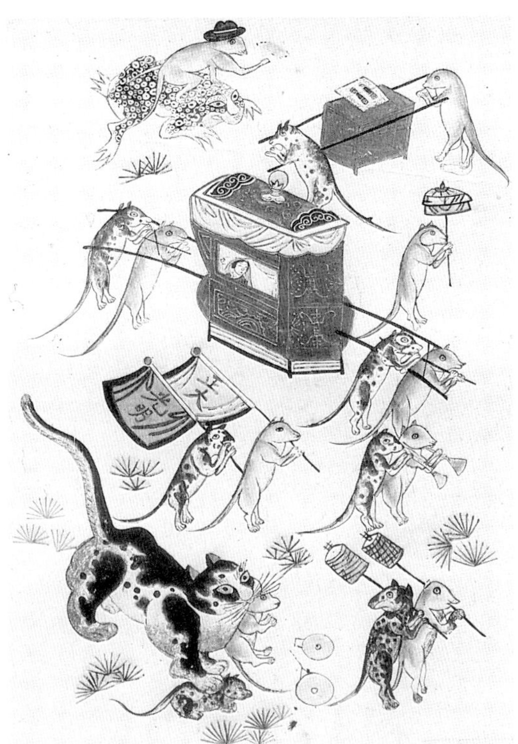

Mouse Marries Daughter, Sichuan

shape. Regardless of the faithful representation of real life, the use of color can be bold and exaggerated. Of course, due to the variety of folk customs and regional characteristics of China, the choices of colors in New Year paintings are also different. For example, vibrant red colors are common in the paintings of north China, while lighter and elegant colors are common in those paintings produced in the south.

It is common to use the expressive skills of symbolism and analogy in the creation of folk arts, especially in New Year paintings. This is to use concrete images to represent abstract concepts, or even to create some abstract symbols for further expression. For instance, the

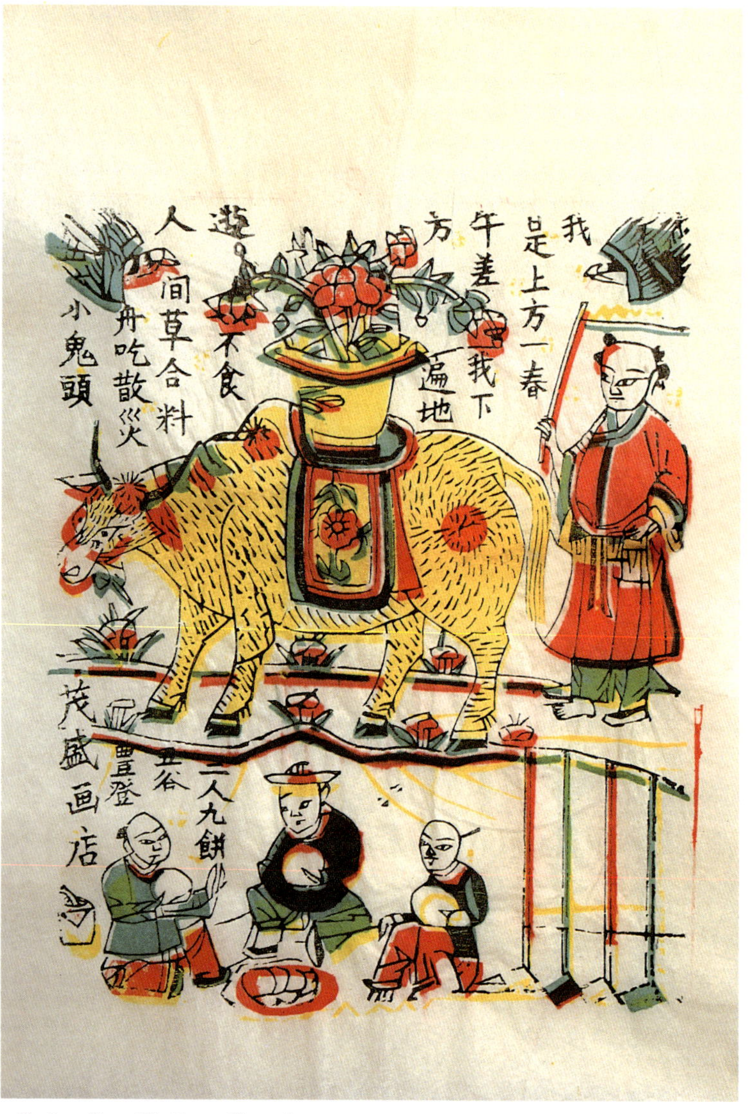

Spring Cow, Xinjiang, Shanxi

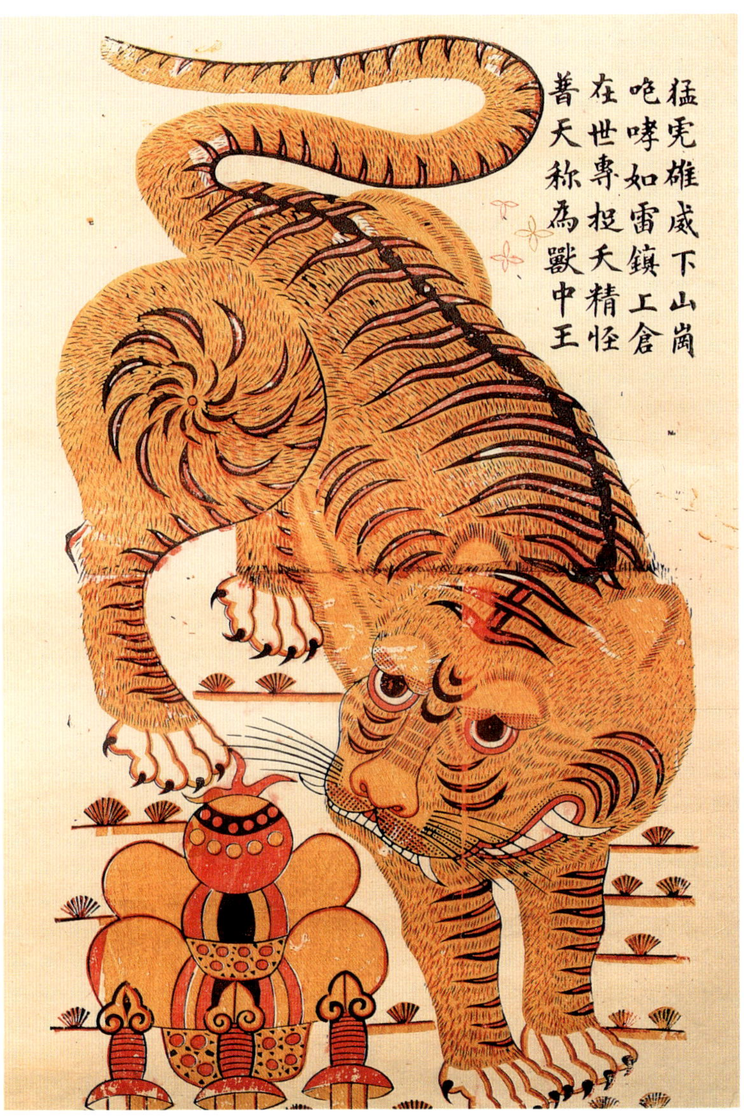

Tiger, Weixian, Shandong

peony flower symbolizes riches and honor; while the peach, crane, pine and *lingzhi* (glossy ganoderma) symbolize longevity; the pomegranate symbolizes fertility; the dragon, phoenix, and Qilin symbolize auspiciousness. Synonyms are often used to express auspicious meanings. Common phonetic sounds are used to symbolize something auspicious. For example, the second character of "bian fu" (bat) sounds like good luck ("fu"), the first character of "shou tao" (peach) sounds like long life ("shou"), so five bats and one peach are painted on the painting to symbolize good luck and longevity. The character "lian" (lotus) sounds like continuous ("lian"), and the character "yu" (fish) sounds like surplus ("yu"), the painting of a fish and a lotus symbolizes "surplus every year."

Other examples include: bottle ("ping"), musical instrument ("sheng") and halberd ("ji") are similar to the slogan, "promoted for three levels"; while three rams ("yang") symbolize "three suns shine." Other methods include symbolic analogies to represent goodwill and good wishes. Certain paintings of figures, mythological stories, and children also use this type of analogy.

Another unique feature of New Year paintings is displaying poetry or notable slogans. Some of these include: "Long life and good harvest," "Happy celebration of the New Year," and "Happiness of the whole family," etc. Some titles are simple and concise, directly explaining the meaning of the painting, such as *The Water Submerging Golden Hill*; *Number One Scholar Grovels Before the Pagoda*; *The Day of Dragon Boat Festival*; *and Stealing Herbs on Fairy Hill*, etc. Some of these are influenced by folk songs, storytelling, fiction, and legendary tales.

New Year paintings featuring prose are simple, unlike scholarly paintings which can be difficult to appreciate. Chinese prose does not have any universal fixed patterns. Some feature three characters per line, some four, some five, some seven, and others ten. All share a unique rhythm and sense of symmetry and balance. For instance, the poem on a painting entitled *Spring Cow* produced in southern Shanxi reads:

I'm a cow from heaven.
Jade Emperor ordered me to travel the earth.
I do not eat grass or fodder.

Only the devils of calamity.

The poem on another painting entitled *Tiger Down the Hill*, produced at Weifang reads:

The mighty tiger goes down the hill.
Its growl shakes the heaven like thunder.
It comes to catch monsters from heaven.
And thus is called the King of Beasts.

The poem on a poster entitled *Lady of Silkworm*, produced in Shandong reads:

The mulberries flourish at the foot of the wall.
The lady picks mulberry leaves and feeds silkworms.
People eat mulberry fruits which are sweet,
While silkworms eat mulberry leaves making silk.

The artistic features of Chinese New Year paintings consist of plain composition, straightforward visualization, and are true to life in how they represent the collective thoughts of society. In its developmental history of more than a thousand years, Chinese New Year painting has developed through periods of prosperity and decline. As a medium of popular culture, it has not only expressed the aesthetic sensibilities and cultural values of the Chinese people, but it has also preserved their social history in vivid form.

Chronological Table of Chinese Dynasties

Five August Emperors	c.30th-21st century B.C.
Xia Dynasty	c.21st-16th century B.C.
Shang Dynasty	c.16th-11th century B.C.
Zhou Dynasty	c.11th century-221 B.C.
Western Zhou Dynasty	c.11th century-771 B.C.
Eastern Zhou Dynasty	770-256 B.C.
Spring and Autumn Period	770-476 B.C.
Warring States Period	475-221 B.C.
Qin Dynasty	221-207 B.C.
Han Dynasty	206 B.C.-A.D. 220
Western Han Dynasty	206 B.C.-A.D. 23
Eastern Han Dynasty	A.D. 25-220
Three Kingdoms Period	220-280
Jin Dynasty	265-420
Western Jin Dynasty	265-316
Eastern Jin Dynasty	317-420
Southern and Northern Dynasties	420-589
Sui Dynasty	581-618
Tang Dynasty	618-907
Five Dynasties	907-960
Song Dynasty	960-1279
Northern Song Dynasty	960-1127
Southern Song Dynasty	1127-1279
Liao Dynasty	916-1125
Kin Dynasty	1115-1234
Yuan Dynasty	1271-1368
Ming Dynasty	1368-1644
Qing Dynasty	1644-1911

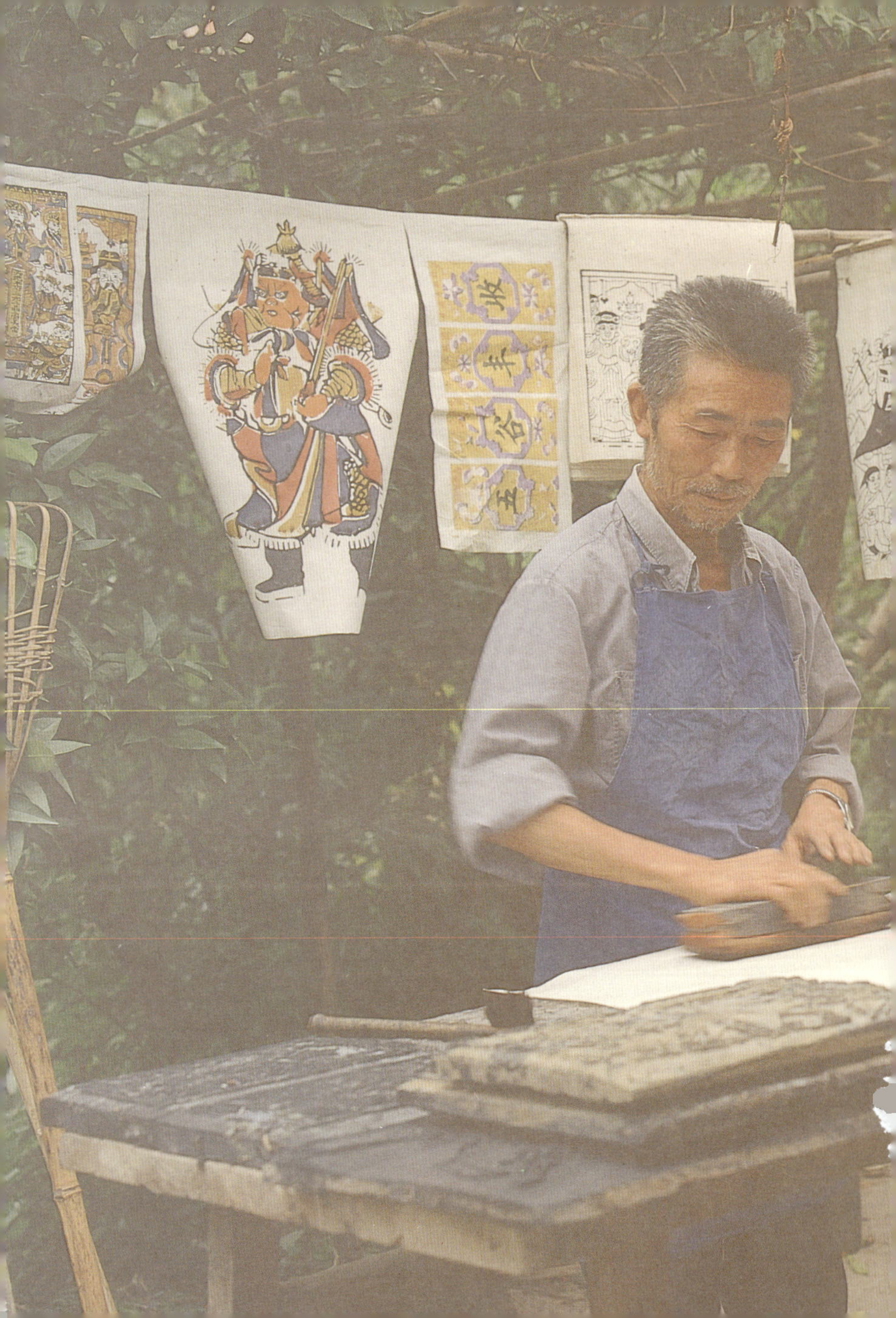
收
丰
谷
五